The Effective Trustee

Aims and Resources

by Kevin Ford

The Effective Trustee

Part One: Roles and Responsibilities
Part Two: Aims and Resources
Part Three: Getting the Work Done

A DIRECTORY OF SOCIAL CHANGE PUBLICATION

**The EFFECTIVE Trustee
Part Two:
Aims and Resources**

A practical guide for charity trustees and members of management committees of voluntary organisations

by Kevin Ford

Published by the **Directory of Social Change**
Radius Works, Back Lane, London, NW3 1HL, 071-435 8171.

Designed and typeset by Tony Goodman

© Directory of Social Change 1993
The Directory of Social Change is an educational charity.
Registration No 800517

No part of this book may be reproduced in any form whatsoever without prior permission in writing from the publisher. Permission will normally be given free of charge to non-profit making and charitable organisations.

Printed and bound in Britain. ISBN 1-873860-23-4

Kevin Ford

Kevin Ford is an independent consultant who has specialised in work with voluntary and charitable organisations. He has worked with a large number of managing committees on issues ranging from induction to resolving conflict. In 1991/92 he completed research on the training needs of charity trustees for the Charity Commissioners and NCVO. He lives in Leicester and is himself a trustee.

Acknowledgements

My thanks to **Michael Norton** for his inspired editing, and to **Kate Sayer, Hilary Richmond** and **Philip Hope** for their comments on the draft.

This book has been produced with generous support from Barclays Bank PLC. The book has been published by the Directory of Social Change. Barclays Bank PLC does not necessarily share the views expressed nor do they accept responsibility for the accuracy of the information or for any expenses or losses caused as a result thereof.

Barclays Bank has a substantial and wide-ranging programme of community support which focuses on charitable donations and sponsorships, secondment of staff, employment initiatives as well as support for environmental projects and the arts.

Barclays believes the most effective way of channelling its charitable support is to target the specific needs of those who are young, elderly, disabled or disadvantaged. Other priority areas for charitable support are medical research and education.

Readers should consult their professional advisers if they deem this to be necessary before entering into any legal commitments.

Contents

1　About this book　*4*

2　Planning what you do　*6*

Making policy • Objects • Statement of aims • Setting objectives and targets
Strategic planning • Priorities • Keeping an overview

3　Accounting for your organisation　*18*

Reporting and accounting requirements • Monitoring and evaluation
Management information • Reporting • Annual report • Promotion

4　Managing your finances　*28*

Legal responsibilities • Accounting principles • Annual accounts • Solvency
Budgets • Management accounts • Independent examination of accounts
VAT • Insurance

5　Managing your assets　*46*

Legal responsibilities • Equipment • Property • Stock • Cash • Investments

6　Fundraising　*52*

Legal responsibilities • Appeal and fundraising committees • Plans
Fundraising strategy • Methods • Asking for money • Tax effective giving

7　Resources　*61*

Booklist • Useful addresses • Useful information

Index　*64*

Chapter 1

About this book

A practical handbook

Our aim in writing this handbook is to help you in your work as a trustee or managing committee member. This book covers two key themes: your organisation's aims and the resources you need to achieve them. It will help you to make sure that your organisation knows exactly where it is going and what it should be doing, and that it uses its resources to best effect. It provides clear, up to date information and ideas for good practice.

Your role as a managing committee member falls into two parts: you have a legal responsibility to see that your organisation operates properly, which we describe as your **trustee responsibilities**; and you have a **management responsibility** for ensuring your organisation does its work to best effect. Throughout this book we draw your attention to these two aspects of your role.

The book includes a variety of checklists and activities to make it as easy as possible to put ideas in to practice. Each chapter ends with a short self-assessment exercise.

Part of a series

"The Effective Trustee: Aims and Resources" is the second in a series of three handbooks from the Directory of Social Change. Some topics mentioned in this book are covered in greater depth in the other two titles: *"Roles and Responsibilities"* and *"Getting the work done"*. Details of their contents are given in the box below.

The series does not aim to be comprehensive. Suggestions for further reading are provided at appropriate points for those who wish to explore the ideas in greater depth. These take the form of a reference to a book number, such as: (*Book 4*), which can be found in the booklist in *Chapter 7*, where there is also a list of useful information.

Who is it for?

If you are involved as a member of the managing committee of a charity, voluntary organisation or community group, or are thinking of getting involved, this handbook is for you.

What's in this book for you?

Reading this book will help you to make sure that you know exactly what you should be doing. You and the other members of your managing committee will be able to ensure that your organisation has clear aims, effective systems of management and that you are using your resources to best possible effect.

This will help your organisation to carry out its work even better, providing more or better quality services and achieving more of your objectives. One result for you will be a greater sense of satisfaction and purpose in your work with the organisation.

The Effective Trustee Series:
Main contents of Parts 1 and 3

The Effective Trustee Part 1
Roles and Responsibilities

1. The legal structures and charitable status of your organisation.

2. The role of your organisation.

3. The role of your managing committee.
   The difference between management and trusteeship.

4. The roles and responsibilities of trustees and managing committee members.

5. Special roles: Officers and Representatives.

6. Recruiting new trustees.

7. Effective committees and ideal trustees.

The Effective Trustee Part 3
Getting the work done

1. Organising your meetings.

2. Working with staff and volunteers.

3. Getting the right people.

4. Managing your premises.

5. Dealing with crises.

6. Working with your membership and users.

7. Getting the most from being a trustee.

Chapter 2

Planning what you do

Your responsibilities

NEED TO KNOW

The managing committee is responsible for making sure that your organisation has clear aims and direction. This is especially important when resources are limited. Your organisation cannot do everything, so you should concentrate on doing what is most important.

Your TRUSTEE responsibilities are to see that your organisation:

- Pursues its objects as set out in the governing instrument;
- Uses its resources cost effectively;
- Operates in the best interests of the beneficiaries;
- Operates only in the area of benefit.

Your MANAGEMENT responsibilities are to see that the organisation has:

- A statement of aims or mission;
- Policies to provide a framework for its work;
- Clear objectives to work towards;
- A strategy to achieve its objectives;
- Discussed and agreed its most important priorities.

The managing committee must make sure that the organisation is true to the values and the spirit which led to its establishment in the first place.

The need

Your organisation was set up to tackle or respond to a need. The trustees should ensure that the organisation does not lose sight of the need. Make sure that you maintain enough information on the need so that you are aware of whether and how it is changing. To do this you should ensure that your organisation listens to the views of its users, members, beneficiaries etc. on a regular basis.

The objects of your organisation

Every organisation has a governing instrument which sets out its objects. These summarise what the organisation was set up to do. These may be very narrow e.g. to provide drinking fountains in schools and public places in London (Metropolitan Drinking Fountain and Cattle Trough Association) or very broad e.g. the advancement of non-academic education (Winston

Policy and Planning Terms explained

TERM	EXPLANATION	EXAMPLE: Midlands Homelessness Trust
Need	The issues or problems that the organisation was set up to tackle.	People unable to afford a place to live in a midlands city.
Values	The values and principles which underpin and guide the work of the organisation.	The trust believes that every person should have access to housing adequate to their needs, and that homelessness is damaging and degrading to those that it affects.
Objects	The purposes of your organisation, as set out in the governing instrument.	The trust's objects are to relieve poverty and distress among the adults of the city and its hinterland, by the provision of residential accommodation.
Aims	What you are aiming to achieve, in the long term. Everything you do should help you to move towards achieving one or more of your aims.	To provide enough good-standard accommodation in the city, so that no-one need sleep rough. To enable people to move on from temporary housing into affordable permanent homes.
Mission	A short statement of what the organisation aims to do, for whom where and how.	The trust works to provide accommodation and support services for any person in the Midlands who is homeless and unable to gain access to anywhere suitable to live.
Policies	Statements which provide a framework for how to respond to particular situations or circumstances.	The trust has an equal opportunities policy, a policy on how to work with its users and a staff development policy.
Objectives	These are more specific than the aims. They tell you in more detail precisely what you intend to achieve, in the short to medium term. An objective should be specific, measurable, achievable, and conform to the aims and values of your organisation. Objectives list the results (sometimes called outputs) your organisation intends to achieve.	The objectives are: • To provide a soup kitchen for people sleeping rough. • To provide information and advice on housing. • To establish housing with appropriate support for people unable to live fully and independently. • To provide low rent flats for single, young people returning to the community from institutions. • To provide medical care for people sleeping rough.
Targets	These identify in detail the things you intend to have done, by a particular date.	The targets are: • To find out what services are currently provided to people on the streets by GPs and health centres, in the city, by conducting a short research study, by November 30th. • To set up a pilot project for one year providing a mobile GP and nurse for one day per week in the Lowater area of the City.
Methods	The ways in which you will seek to achieve your objectives. They include programmes, services, activities etc. They are the things you will do to get the results you want.	*This example shows how targets often include a description of the method (how the work will be done).*

"Aims", "objectives", "goals", "targets" are often used loosely and interchangeably. This can cause confusion. We can distinguish between these different words, on the basis of the timescale involved. Aims are very long term; objectives can be both long and shorter term, goals and targets are short term. For more detail see Books 1 and 2.

Changing your objects

The circumstances in which a charity's objects can be changed are set out in the Charities Act.

In summary these are:

- where the original purposes have either been fulfilled or can no longer be carried out;
- where the original purposes use only part of the property given by a donor (as in the case of charity which is given land, whose value increases dramatically and provides more income than can be distributed according to the objects);
- where the original area of benefit no longer exists or the beneficiaries are no longer suitable (e.g. charities which were set up to benefit spinsters may widen their objects to cover poor people in the area);
- where the original objects are now provided for by other means (as in the case of services now provided by the State, such as repairing bridges).

You should professional advice or consult the Charity Commissioners before setting out to change your objects.

Constitutional Objects

CHECK POINT

- Have you read and understood the objects, beneficiaries and area of benefit of your organisation?

- Are the objects still achievable in the present day?

- Has your organisation interpreted the objects to bring them up to date with modern needs?

- Is the interpretation in line with the original objects and/or with your founder's intentions?

- Do you really need to change any of your objects? If so, are you aware of the procedure you must adopt to do this?

Churchill Memorial Trust). Your organisation is only allowed to operate within its constitutional objects.

In older organisations, the objects may be written in archaic language, or refer to needs which have changed over time.

For example, a Victorian charity set up to protect girls in moral danger (servants at risk of molestation by their masters) might be interpreted in modern terms to allow its involvement in women's aid, rape crisis and so on.

Or a charity set up to assist poor apprentices to buy the tools of their trades might be interpreted to allow for the education and training of young people in the area of benefit.

The trustees or managing committee members must make sure that the objects are understood, and that they are interpreted in a way which makes them relevant to present day needs.

The beneficiaries and area of benefit

The governing instrument sets out the people who will benefit from the work of your organisation: the beneficiaries; and the area you are allowed to work in: the area of benefit. This may be local, national or international. The terms used may be old-fashioned. For example, a local area of benefit may be an historic parish which no longer exists, having been swallowed up by a larger town.

You, and the other managing committee members must make sure that you know who your organisation's beneficiaries are, and what your area of benefit is.

Changing your objects

If your organisation is not a charity it is free to change its governing instrument, provided it follows the procedure for such changes set out in the governing instrument. If your organisation is a charity, it is more difficult to change its objects. The following steps should be taken.

1. Check first that you really do need to change the objects. If the language is interpreted in a modern way, are your original objects still relevant? Is there still a need for you to meet?
(If you have any doubt about interpretation of your organisation's objects, always check with the Charity Commissioners.)

2. Look in your governing instrument to see whether your organisation has the power to change its objects. If so, follow the procedure laid down, and submit the changes to the Charity Commissioners for approval.

3. If the objects must be changed because they can no longer be fulfilled, and your governing instrument does not give any power to the trustees to change them, your organisation can apply to the Charity Commissioners for a cy-pres scheme. "Cy-pres" means "as near as possible". The objects can be changed only as much as is necessary to give effect to the original general intentions of the donor.

4. If you are a limited company or an industrial and provident society, you will need to ensure that any changes you make to your objects are acceptable to the relevant registrar.

Small charities

The 1992 Charities Act increased the powers of trustees of small, local charities to manage their own affairs. The trustees of charities with an annual income of less than £5,000 can:

- Transfer property to one or more charities with similar purposes;
- Amend their objects or modify the provisions of the trust deed.

Trustees of charities with an annual gross income of less than £1,000 and which have a permanent endowment, have the power to spend their capital, if

---

Map your vision

On a large piece of paper, draw a picture or a diagram of what your organisation would be like if it was doing everything you think it should be doing and it had sufficient resources to do it? Let yourself go and use your imagination.

Share your ideas with the other trustees. Are you of one mind? What are the differences? Can you construct a collective picture of where the organisation is going?

ACTIVITY

they are satisfied that the income it produces is too small to be of practical value. In all the above cases, trustees must decide to take the actions by at least a two-thirds majority. They must also give public notice of their intentions, and secure the agreement of the Charity Commissioners.

The aims

The managing committee should share a vision of what it would be like if the organisation achieved everything you wanted it to achieve. This gives your organisation its aims for and provides purpose and direction. This may seem to be ideal, but our dreams can inspire and motivate us. This vision can capture the values and hopes which drive your organisation forward.

Setting clear aims

Charities and voluntary organisations exist to pursue their objects, which are set out in their governing instruments. One of the most important management tasks of the managing committee is to translate the objects into a clear, understandable set of aims. The aims are what the organisation intends to achieve in the long term.

You should make sure that the aims are:
- In accord with your objects;
- Clear and understood;
- Shared by everyone involved with the organisation;
- Kept up to date.

The aims answer the question "why" when applied to any of the organisation's activities. They give coherence and purpose to everything that the organisation does. If an organisation loses sight of its aims, sooner or later it will lose its way.

Statements of aims or mission

Many organisations write a statement of their aims or mission. This is a short, clear statement of what the organisation aims to do, for whom, where and how. It includes the methods you use and how you judge the quality of your work.

Why have a mission statement?

Your mission statement provides a short, easily understood summary of what your organisation is all about. It provides a unifying focus for everyone involved with the organisation.

If it is written in a lively, memorable way, it will help communicate the essence of your organisation. Use the statement on all your publicity material, reports, publications and so on. It can help to establish your image and keep your organisation in people's minds.

Example statements of aims or mission

MacIntyre, a national charity concerned with people with mental disabilities has the following mission:
MacIntyre is a network of residential, daycare and occupational resources in England and Wales dedicated to enabling children and adults who have a mental disability to overcome the factors which handicap them.

Methodist Homes for the Aged states its mission as:
to provide a range of accommodation and care services, based on Christian principles, which are open to all elderly people in need, whatever their beliefs.

Whether you call it a statement of aims or mission, your organisation should have an agreed statement which explains:
- Who you are;
- What you do (your aims, drawn from your constitutional objects);
- The principles underlying what you do;
- Who you work with or for (your beneficiaries);
- Where you work (your area of benefit).

Examples of policies in voluntary organisations
- Statements of principles or values which underlie the work.
- Aims, objectives and priorities provide an overall framework for your organisation's activities.
- Policies relating to the employment of staff.
- Equal opportunity policies.
- Ethical or moral policies - such as a medical charity having a policy not to invest in the tobacco industry.
- Financial policies giving a framework for managing the finances.
- Policy to deal with conflict and crisis.

Policy
CHECK POINT
- What policies does your organisation currently have?
- Who decides what policies your organisation has?
- What principles lie behind these policies?
- Are the policies clear and understandable?
- Do you have plans for implementing the policies?

Making policy

Policies give organisations broad frameworks within which to operate. They define what an organisation should be doing, in general or in response to a particular situation, and the way it should be done.

Policies give stability to organisations, as everyone involved can refer back to the policy for guidance on how best to proceed. The managing committee plays a vital role in making sure that your organisation has suitable policies.

Objectives

Your organisation's aims can be broken down into more specific, shorter-term objectives. These are the things that you will be doing to pursue your aims.
It is important that the objectives focus on results. After all, the organisation will be judged on what it has done.

Targets

Each objective breaks down into shorter term targets. These are more specific, and should be measurable, so that progress can be assessed.

Putting policy into practice

PRACTICAL POINTER

You are responsible for the overall direction of your organisation. How do you make sure that your policies are put into practice? There are several levels at which you can work.

▶ The managing committee receives regular reports on progress and policy and may organise a special meeting to review the strategy (perhaps annually).

▶ Sub-committees meet to focus on particular aspects of the organisation's work. These may have more involvement with day to day activities.

▶ Contact with staff and volunteers, such as holding meetings to explain and discuss the organisation's policies.

▶ Contact with the work of the organisation as a volunteer, or through visits to projects or sites.

▶ Contact with the clients and users of services, through meetings or using questionnaires etc.

▶ A general interest in the cause and in what others are doing and thinking.

Aims and objectives

CHECK POINT

- What are the aims of your organisation?
- When did your organisation last discuss its aims? Do you need to bring them up to date, or amend them in any way?
- Does your organisation have a short, memorable mission statement or statement of aims? How is this statement used?
- What are the objectives of your organisation?
- Do you and the other trustees review progress towards each objective, on a regular basis? When and how is this done?
- Do your objectives reflect your policies and your aims?
- Does your organisation have adequate systems to translate your objectives into realistic, measurable targets? Who does this? How is progress reported back to the managing committee?

The Effective Trustee

TECHNICAL DETAIL

Types of planning

Strategic planning:	long term; broad overview of policies; longer term objectives; major activities; new developments and use of resources
Tactical or operational planning:	steps to put the long term plans into action
Day to day planning:	specific actions to put the operational plans into action on a daily basis
Regular planning:	planning for the annual cycle of events (such as funding applications)
Crisis planning:	reacting to events as they happen

A target should be "SMART":

- **S**pecific
- **M**easurable
- **A**chievable
- **R**elated to a longer term objective and an aim
- **T**imed (i.e. a date set for achieving it)

These targets should again focus on results (outputs). By seeing that there are clear aims, objectives and targets the managing committee has a framework against which the progress of the organisation can be measured, as well as an effective way to check that it is not straying from its constitutional objects.

Strategic planning

Planning is essential to achieving success in most activities. We all do it, whether formally or informally. Trustees play a vital management role in the overall planning of their organisation's work. The most important aspect of this is planning for the long term, and keeping a broad overview of the use of resources, major activities and new developments. This is strategic planning.

A strategic plan:

- Takes a **long-term view** (one to five years),
- Focuses on **what the organisation will do**, why and very broadly, how,
- Relates the whole organisation to **the world around it**,
- Takes account of the **resources needed**, and which must be obtained.

"Strategic planning is the process by which the guiding members of an organisation envision its future and develop the necessary procedures and operations to achieve that future" (*Shaping Strategic Planning*, Pfeiffer et al, University Associates, 1989)

The strategic plan should be a short document. It will help you to direct and

CHECK POINT

Strategic planning

- Who does the planning in your organisation?
- What sort of planning does the managing committee get involved in?
- Does your managing committee succeed in keeping a broad strategic overview of your organisation's work?
- Does your organisation have a strategic plan?
- When was it drawn up?
- Who was involved in drawing it up?
- Did trustees, staff, volunteers and users all contribute to the drafting of the plan?
- Is it clear and realistic?
- When will it be reviewed?
- Does your managing committee delegate shorter term matters effectively to staff?

The Effective Trustee

Drawing up a strategic plan:

1. Review the **main achievements and weaknesses** of your organisation over the last year. This should include the views of staff, volunteers and users of your services.
   What have you done really well? What were the results of your work? What were your major successes? What changes did you achieve?
   What were you unable to do, or did not do as well as you would have liked? Why?
   What stage of growth has your organisation reached? Is it new, well established, dying?

2. Write down **what you want to achieve** in the next year or so. This will include your aims (very broad) and more specific objectives. These objectives should focus on the results you want to achieve.

3. List all **the factors that might help** you to achieve this (eg funding, government support, changes in the law, changes in public awareness, staffing, resources, volunteers, premises, equipment etc).
   List all the factors that might hinder your progress.
   Look ahead. Take into account any changes in the outside world which are likely to have an effect on your organisation.

4. Write down **what you will have to do** if you are to achieve what you want and the main resources you will need to do this. Be realistic. Do not plan on the basis of resources you are unlikely to be able to get.

5. Identify **how you will judge** your performance. What will constitute success?

ACTIVITY

organise your work. It will help you to identify which areas of work are most important - have highest priority. It will also identify those issues where more detailed thinking is needed.

Good planning helps to prevent the organisation from sitting back and waiting for things to happen. It means that you are ready and properly prepared to meet any challenges which arise in your work, rather than lurching from one crisis to another.

Although the trustees have particular responsibility for the strategic planning, it is very important that you make use of the expertise and experience of your staff, volunteers and the users of your services in drawing up your plans. Taking part in the planning can help to build commitment towards the work of the organisation.

Strategic Planning

Keep your strategic plan in mind by regularly asking the following questions about any of your activities:

▶ **Is the activity in line with your strategy?**

▶ **How much priority should the organisation be giving it?**

▶ **Should the organisation be doing it at all?**

▶ **What progress is the organisation making towards achieving its strategy? How do you measure this?**

PRACTICAL POINTER

The Effective Trustee

> **Example: Keeping to your priorities**
>
> An environmental group agreed, as a priority, to set up a wild-life garden in a run-down area of the inner city.
>
> After six months the project had gained strong local support, and the backing of the council, plus various offers of help.
>
> As a result of this success, representatives from three other local communities approached the trustees to ask for similar projects in their areas. The trustees considered each request, but said no to each, adding that they hoped to be able to help one new project in the next financial year. They explained that the organisation simply did not have the resources to do more than this.
>
> Setting clear priorities enabled the organisation to limit its activities and to focus energy on achieving an impact in one area. If other work had been taken one, the chances are that resources would have been spread too thin, and results would have been poor.

Setting priorities

Few organisations ever have sufficient resources to do all the work they would like to do. All have to make sure that they apply their limited resources effectively. This means agreeing which areas of work are the most important, concentrating your resources there, and ensuring that the work is of high quality and has an impact.

Deciding to concentrate on doing one thing rather than something else involves setting priorities.

Agreeing priorities means that you can decide how best to allocate your resources, time, and energy. It also means that you are better able to say "no" to ideas or activities lie outside your priorities.

Different organisations set their priorities in different ways. A community transport service might have a fairly stable set of priorities. A neighbourhood association may want to retain a greater level of flexibility, so that it can deal with new issues as they arise.

Planning should never be so rigid that it prevents an organisation from responding to new needs.

Day-to-day planning

The managing committee, with advice from staff, sets the framework within

CHECK POINT

Priorities

- Does your organisation have a clear set of priorities?

- Are new ideas for your organisation's work discussed in relation to your existing priorities?

- Does your organisation stick to its priorities?

- Are the priorities reviewed on a regular basis? If so, how and when?

- Who decides on the priorities? - What is the role of staff in setting priorities? What involvement do clients and consumers of your services have in influencing the choice of priorities.

The Effective Trustee

The division of responsibilities between trustees, sub-committees and paid staff.

TECHNICAL DETAIL

Task	Responsibility
Interpreting the objects	Managing Committee
Agreeing values	Managing committee with input from all who have an interest in the organisation. Ensures appropriate framework for the activities of the organisation.
Establishing clear aims	Managing committee, with the involvement of staff, volunteers and users.
Writing a mission statement	Managing committee, with advice from staff. Volunteers and users should be consulted.
Strategic planning	Managing committee and key staff (Director and Management Team). Committee responsible, staff advisory. Sets and monitors broad policies and goals. Time span 1-5 years
Shorter term planning	Delegated to key staff and sub-committees who work to the framework of the strategic plan. Emphasis is on specific, achievable objectives and targets. Time span three months - one year
Specific work planning	Delegated to individual staff or volunteers who are responsible for getting the work done.

In small organisations with no or few paid staff, managing committee members may play all three roles: firstly to devise the strategic plan, and secondly to draw up shorter term plans, and lastly to put the plans in to action as active volunteers.

Example: Keeping an overview

The Board of Trustees of the Night Shelter were having to meet more and more frequently. Meetings were getting longer and most of the time was being spent on detailed day-to-day management such as: deciding what sort of computer to buy, editing a new promotional leaflet, discussing the best people to ask to speak at the AGM, dealing with staff problems.

The co-ordinator was becoming increasingly frustrated, as almost every decision seemed to need to be ratified by the Board. She felt she was not being trusted to get on with the job. The trustees complained that they could no longer see the wood for the trees, and that they could not cope with the amount of work they were being asked to do. They had lost sight of the overall purpose of the organisation. Decisions were being made in reaction to crises rather than as part of a purposeful plan.

After a discussion of the problems, the trustees agreed that they must get a clearer focus on the overview of the organisation. Day-to-day matters would be delegated to a new Executive Sub-Committee. This would report its decisions to the board. The decisions would only be re-opened for discussion in exceptional circumstances.

The Executive Sub-Committee agreed that most day-to-day decisions should be delegated to the co-ordinator. They would discuss only the more major decisions. The co-ordinator should report on a monthly basis to the Executive sub-committee.

The Effective Trustee

PRACTICAL POINTER

Focus on wider matters

▶ Keep the managing committee's agenda focused on the overview of the organisation - the strategic plan, your mission and overall aims.

▶ Don't let the committee get bogged down in day to day detail. If you find too much time is being spent on everyday matters - delegate more to staff or to sub-committees.

▶ Make sure that you delegate well. You must trust the staff or sub-committees to make decisions and instigate action. They in turn must report back to you. If you find that your committee is repeating everything that was agreed by the staff or sub-committee, then you have not delegated properly.

which staff and volunteers can draw up more detailed plans for the day-to-day activities of the organisation.

Many managing committees delegate the detailed planning of day-to-day work to a sub-committee, staff or both. The managing committee is then able to maintain a clear overview of the wider aspects of the organisation and how it is progressing.

In organisations which employ paid staff, most of the planning is done by them. The task is usually delegated to the Director and the management team. S/he may work closely with a sub-committee, such as an Executive Committee. Delegation does not mean losing interest. Trustees must make sure they receive reports, and should review progress on a regular (possibly an annual) basis.

Where no paid staff are employed, the trustees may find themselves involved more directly in the day-to-day planning. They will usually do this through sub-committees or working groups.

The planning process converts the organisation's vision into smaller, specific targets which can be achieved over a given time span - such as the next year. It allocates work to particular individuals or departments, along with the resources to do it.

Self-assessment

Accounting for your organisation

		Know	Must check
1.	What are the differences between objects, aims and objectives?	☐	☐
2.	How do the aims of an organisation relate to its vision of where it is going?	☐	☐
3.	Why do organisations have policies?	☐	☐
4.	Who should decide which policies your organisation should have?	☐	☐
5.	What should be included in an effective statement of aims or mission?	☐	☐
6.	How would you translate your organisation's objectives into targets?	☐	☐
7.	What sort of planning should your managing committee focus upon?	☐	☐
8.	How would you draw up a strategic plan?	☐	☐
9.	Why are priorities important?	☐	☐
10.	Who should decide your organisation's priorities?	☐	☐

Chapter 3

Accounting for your organisation

Your responsibilities:

NEED TO KNOW

The managing committee is responsible for making sure that your organisation accounts for its activities to others. This is important not only in satisfying funders that your organisation is effective, but also in explaining the organisation to a wider audience.

Your TRUSTEE responsibilities are to fulfill all the legal requirements for reporting on and accounting for the work of your organisation

Your MANAGEMENT responsibilities are to ensure that:

- **The work of the organisation is effective. You should see that it is properly monitored and is evaluated on a regular basis;**
- **The managing committee is kept fully in touch. You should be receiving reports on current work, financial reports, and relevant information on assets, premises and equipment;**
- **Your organisation reports its progress to people with an interest in it. This includes members, clients, consumers and the wider community that benefits from your activities.**

Reporting and accounting requirements

You, with the other managing committee members, are responsible for reporting to:

- The Charity Commissioners (if your organisation is a registered charity);
- The Registrar of Companies (if your organisation is a company limited by guarantee) or the Register of Friendly Societies (if your organisation is an industrial and provident society);
- Your members (if you are required to do so in your constitution);
- Your funders: local authority, trusts and other donors (if you are required to do so under the terms of your grants or donations).

The exact reporting requirements are spelled out by each body. Failure to report accurately and on time may place the trustees at risk of prosecution.

Registered charities must submit an annual report to the Charity Commissioners (if based in England or Wales), which will include:

- A statement of accounts, together with the auditor's or independent examiner's report;
- An annual return giving details of the trustees;
- The trustees' report on the activities of the charity during the year.

Charities in Scotland must produce a similar report, which must be made available on request.

Companies limited by guarantee must also submit, to the Registrar of Companies:

- An annual report from the directors;
- Audited accounts;
- An annual return giving details of directors.

The above reports must be sent at specified times. For example, a charity's accounts must be submitted within ten months of the end of the organisation's financial year.

Reports to funders

Many funders make it a condition of their grant that they receive an annual report and accounts from your organisation within a specified time.

It is the responsibility of the managing committee to make sure that proper reports and accounts are provided as per the terms of grant. For more detail see *Book 4*.

Monitoring and evaluating the work

You need to know what work has been done. You need to be sure that all the work done by the organisation is in line with its charitable objects, and is using your resources efficiently. You should be able to judge the impact and effectiveness of the work done.

Monitoring involves recording what has been done and what has happened, and checking this against what was intended to happen (as in your plans).

Evaluation is the process of judging the value of your organisation's work and deciding whether it has been effective.

Your organisation will need to have a good, reliable system for recording relevant information, for monitoring the work, for measuring achievements and for accounting for the money you have spent. It is up to the trustees to make sure such systems exist and are used.

Example: Monitoring and evaluation

A small rural transport scheme

Records:
journeys undertaken, mileage, passengers carried, vehicle costs, petrol used, volunteer involvement, staffing costs, punctuality, safety, breakdown of passengers by age, race, gender, disability, etc.

Monitors:
progress towards its objective to provide transport to local people with poor access to public transport and no transport of their own. This includes finding out about the quality of the service - comfort, friendliness, user satisfaction etc.

Evaluates:
the extent and quality of the service; its cost effectiveness and its value to the clients.

The trustees should try to judge the value of the service. What difference has it made to people who have no transport? What impact has it had on their lives? Are the methods used the most effective way of achieving the objective? Is the organisation achieving its aims?

The local authority (which is funding the project) might evaluate solely on a cost per passenger mile basis, and compare the service to, say, a local bus operator. This reflects the different perspective of the authority.

Example

Evaluating advice work

An advice agency might be concerned with the following:

Inputs:
Staff time, volunteer time, running costs.

Process:
Giving advice and information face-to-face, by telephone and through leaflets, and doing this in a friendly, accurate and accessible way.

Outputs:
The number of people advised, broken down by age, gender, race, geographical area etc. The amount of advice given on particular topics (welfare rights, debt, housing etc.). The number of advice leaflets distributed.

Outcomes:
The number of people who are satisfied with the advice received (through asking clients to complete evaluation forms). The number of people who are able to act on advice received and the actual benefits to the clients resulting from the advice given (found out through follow up research).

Your managing committee meetings should allow time to reflect on the organisation's performance and to make sensible judgements about how well you are achieving the purposes of the organisation.

You must ensure that you are receiving appropriate information. Too much will be expensive to collect and bog you down with detail. Too little and you will not be able to make effective judgements about the value of your work.

Outcomes and achievements

Evaluation can look at four aspects of your work:

Inputs: what goes in to the organisation, the resources and effort the organisation spends on its different activities.

Process: the way in which work is done.

Outputs: what is done; the quantity and quality of the services provided (which you can measure from your own records).

Outcomes: the impact of the work done - in meeting the need, solving a problem, creating change (which you will need to find out, usually from the clients or users).

Inputs and process relate to what the people working for your organisation do and the way they do it. Outputs relate to what your organisation does for its clients or consumers. The outcomes show what impact you have made on the needs you set out to tackle. Your achievements in terms of outputs and outcomes are the most important things to focus on. It is vital that the organisation keeps records to give you the required information.

Evaluation

CHECK POINT

- How do you measure the work of your organisation?
- What systems do you use to collect information?
- How is information reported to the trustees?
- When you evaluate, do you discuss both what has been done (inputs and process) and the results (outputs and outcomes)?
- What role do your trustees/managing committee members play in the evaluation process?

What Will Your Organisation Measure

You must be sure that whoever is doing the work is keeping records so that progress can be assessed.

The things you decide to measure give you an indication of how well you are doing. Hence their name: indicators. Below are some examples of indicators you might consider using. Tick the ones which are appropriate to your organisation.

☐ **Number of users:**
total number and the total as a percentage of all possible users.

☐ **Work involved:**
amount of staff time spent on the activity. Amount of volunteer time spent.

☐ **Financial data:**
the total cost of the service. Cost divided by the number of users to give the unit cost. Total sales income or receipts.

☐ **Comparison with other organisations:**
a comparison of unit costs.

☐ **Operating capacity:**
number of hours/days per week the service is available or used with its maximum capacity. Number of people turned away through lack of resources (unmet need).

☐ **Performance against agreed standards:**
time taken to respond to queries.

☐ **Performance against plans:**
have all operating targets in your plan been met? If not, why not?

☐ **User feedback:**
comments from users on the services. Number of complaints and an analysis of them.

☐ **Incident analysis:**
recording a particular event or problem, in detail.

☐ **Monitoring reports:**
through site visits to check what's actually happening.

☐ **Longer term follow-up research:**
contact with users after a period of months or years to determine the outcomes or impact of the work.

☐ **Press coverage:**
number of mentions in the press, radio, TV and any response.

☐ **Other**
....
....
....

Evaluating your organisation's work

Select an example of an area of work carried out by your organisation.
Note down the ways in which the organisation:

Records the work done
Who does it? How? How often? When? Is it easy to compile? Is it the right information? What else could you record?

Reports
what has happened? How is the information produced for trustees? Is it useful?

Monitors progress
How can you use the information to assess progress towards achieving your targets?

Evaluates
what has been achieved? How do you measure outputs and outcomes? Do you need any other information in order to make judgements about the effectiveness of your organisation's work? How can you use your evaluation to improve future quality and performance?

Twelve KEY Features of Evaluation

TECHNICAL DETAIL

1. Judges the worth or **value of the work** done by an organisation.

2. **Looks back** at work done over a period of time.

3. Requires **criteria to judge the work** done. These criteria are based on the values, purposes, objectives and priorities of the organisation.

4. Requires **information** in order **to make informed judgements**. Information comes from two sources: qualitative data (descriptions of what has been done, opinions, views, observations, etc); and quantitative data (facts and figures).

5. Requires **comparisons** so that progress can be measured against plans (the targets set in advance); over a given period of time; in comparison to other projects undertaken by you or by others.

6. Is a **continuous** process. Good evaluation includes observation and judgement of the work by everyone involved and allows those views to be shared, alongside the collection of more systematic information.

7. Requires simple, practical systems of recording data and **gathering information.** There is no point setting up elaborate systems which take up a lot of time or effort and which no-one has time to use.

8. Requires you to **do something**. The process does not just happen - it must be planned into work programmes.

9. Should **include everyone** involved with the organisation. Everybody should have a way of contributing to the evaluation of the work of the organisation. You need systems of feed-back from staff, volunteers, committee members, clients and consumers.

10. Does **not** provide absolute proof of good performance. There is no single set of criteria by which an organisation can be judged. All organisations should develop their own criteria. People outside the organisations may make judgements on a completely different basis.

11. Is **action orientated**. Evaluation provides the basis for informed decisions about how to make the work of the organisation even more effective. It is not separate, occasional activity, but a regular, straightforward part of the everyday running of the organisation.

12. Is part of **the wider planning process**. Many people see evaluation as separate to the process of planning. It is not. It is an essential part of improving your organisation's work and planning its future.

From: Effortless Evaluation, Kevin Ford, Northern Ireland Council for Voluntary Action. 1993.

It is your job, as a trustee, to see not only that your organisation does its work, but that the work has an impact. For further information see *Books 11-13*.

Management information

The managing committee needs to receive enough information about the work of the organisation to make informed judgements about progress and reach good decisions. This is management information. Too much information will overload you. Too little will leave you ill-informed and unable to play your role effectively.

Management information consists of:

- **Quantitative** information (numbers, measurements, etc.), and
- **Qualitative** information (descriptions, opinions, thoughts, etc.),

which have been summarised in order to enable you to make judgements and decisions.

The managing committee should decide what information it wishes to receive from staff and volunteers. It should periodically review whether it is receiving the right information in the right form.

Producing the information

Information can be presented in the following ways, for discussion at committee meetings:

- **The Director's report** on overall progress in relation to plans and targets.
- **A financial report** alongside the management accounts.
- **Short reports** on each main project or area of activity to assure you that everything is going to plan (or not).
- **Reports from sub-committees** on work that was delegated to them.

Management information
CHECK POINT

- How does your organisation gather information about its activities?
- Who collects it? How is it recorded?
- How is information passed on to the managing committee?
- Do you, and the other managing committee members, receive enough information to make decisions about your organisation?
- If not, what additional information do you need?

These reports should not require much further discussion.

- **Agenda item**s, with relevant information (usually as short papers, sometimes verbal information) produced for discussion highlighting specific issues or problems requiring decisions.

After each meeting trustees should know:

- What **progress** has been made and that it is in line with objectives.
- What **problems or issues** have arisen and that they have been dealt with or **decisions** made to deal with them.
- The **financial position** of the organisation.

Working links
PRACTICAL POINTER

▶ Each committee member can be linked up to a particular project or area of the organisation's work. This might involve regular contact with staff and volunteers, or serving on a specialist sub-committee. Each committee member is able to build up specific knowledge for discussion at committee when needed.

▶ In this way all trustees keep an overview, but each has an area of special interest and expertise.

Sources of Information

Many trustees rely mostly on written reports produced for managing committee meetings. More active trustees will want to gather information for themselves by:

- **Visiting projects** or activities and seeing the work at first hand.
- **Talking to staff**, volunteers and service users.
- **Taking part in meetings** which review the work.
- **Keeping informed** about the field of work in general, visiting other similar projects.

This can help to build up a more informed picture of what is going on.

Reporting

The annual report

The main way many organisations report on their work is by producing an Annual Report. Many people regard this as a chore, yet it may be the only information widely available about your organisation. As such it is also a vital promotional and marketing tool. All too few organisations make full use of their annual report.

A good annual report will:

- Contain brief, enthusiastic reports on the work your organisation has done and its achievements during the year;
- Include pertinent facts and figures, certain case studies or descriptions which capture the quality of the activities and services;
- Include a statement of your overall aims and mission;
- Assess progress over the year;
- Contain photographs and diagrams, not just words;
- Include financial information (other than complete or summary accounts);
- List the patrons, trustees and key staff;
- Be lively and readable so that it will be read.

Allocate enough time and resources to produce a report which captures the essence of your organisation, re-enforces the value of the work you are doing and keeps people informed. You can use photographs and case studies (suitably disguised if confidentiality is a requirement) to liven up the report.

Make sure that the report is circulated to members, donors, volunteers and the key people with a stake in your organisation. For more on annual reports, see *Book 7*.

Other ways of reporting

The annual report alone may not be enough to ensure that everyone is kept informed. Other methods of reporting include:

- Producing simple leaflets or brochures for wider circulation.
- Reporting through the local press/radio/TV on particular events and activities which seem newsworthy.
- Writing articles for journals.
- Holding open meetings with members/clients/consumers.
- Reporting **in person** to people with a particular interest (such as funders, major donors).

Larger organisations may employ a specialist press officer, smaller organisations may rely on a particular staff member or volunteer.

Every trustee is a potential ambassador for your organisation. Keeping trustees informed and interested will help enable them to give lively reports to other people they meet.

Reporting and promoting to the public

The managing committee should take steps to ensure that the organisation gets information about itself to the public in general. You are seeking both to provide people with information about what you do, and to get support for your work.

You have two roles:

- As a trustee, to see that the organisation is promoted effectively, that this is done in keeping with its aims and its values.
- As a volunteer, to actually promote and publicise the organisation and its work.

To carry out your trustee role, you need to keep yourself informed about what is being done. You should know the what is being said about the organisation, what methods are employed and what images it is using in its materials. You should also see that the organisation has a strategy for its promotion.

You can provide useful feedback to the committee by using your own contacts to get a picture of how people outside the organisation see it. Is your message getting across to the people you want to reach?

Reporting and promotion

- Who is responsible for producing your organisation's annual report? Does it convey all you would wish to its readers? Could it be improved?

CHECK POINT

- What other ways of reporting does your organisation use? Is the organisation being promoted effectively? How? To whom? For what purpose?
- What messages are being used? What images are being used? Are the messages and images appropriate?
- Is there a promotional strategy? Who is responsible for carrying it out?

The Effective Trustee

Reporting methods

An effective organisation aims to report to all those with an interest in its activities. Tick the methods that your organisation already uses to communicate with its target audiences. Note down any that you think might useful in the future.

Target Group/Method

Service users
- ☐ Personal contact
- ☐ Explanatory leaflets
- ☐ Newsletter
- ☐ Feedback meetings
- ☐ Annual report

Funders
- ☐ Personal contacts
- ☐ Annual report
- ☐ Written reports
- ☐ Field visits and open days

Regulatory
- ☐ Annual report and accounts bodies

Target Group/Method

Staff
- ☐ Staff meetings and briefings
- ☐ Newsletter
- ☐ Personal contact with trustees
- ☐ Annual report

Volunteers
- ☐ Personal contact
- ☐ Volunteers meetings
- ☐ Newsletter
- ☐ Annual report

Trustees
- ☐ Personal contact with staff and volunteers
- ☐ Reports, meetings and trustee field visits

Methods of promotion

- ☐ Word of mouth.
- ☐ Local and national press coverage, in news and feature articles.
- ☐ Specialist and "trade" press coverage.
- ☐ Leaflets.
- ☐ Posters and billboards.
- ☐ Events, such as open days, exhibitions.
- ☐ Coverage on local or national radio and television.
- ☐ Publications.
- ☐ Others: ....
  ....
  ....

Read through the above list. Identify the methods of promotion that your organisation is currently using. Which are most effective? Which are not effective? Why? Identify any other methods you think your organisation should be using.

Discuss your conclusions with the other trustees.

Self-assessment

Accounting for your organisation

		Know	Must check
1.	Who must your organisation report to regarding its work each year?	☐	☐
2.	What is the difference between monitoring and evaluation?	☐	☐
3.	How do you assess the impact your organisation is making on the need it was set up to meet?	☐	☐
4.	What is the difference between an output and an outcome?	☐	☐
5.	Can you list five ways to measure your organisation's performance?	☐	☐
6.	What are the twelve key features of evaluation?	☐	☐
7.	What is management information and how is it used?	☐	☐
8.	What should a good annual report contain?	☐	☐
9.	What is the role of trustees in promoting their organisation?	☐	☐

Chapter 4

Managing your finances

> **Your responsibilities**
>
> *NEED TO KNOW*
>
> The managing committee must make sure that the organisation has sound and healthy finances.
>
> Your TRUSTEE responsibilities are to ensure that:
>
> - All money and assets are used wholly for the objects of your organisation, as spelled out in its governing instrument.
> - Money is used only for the purposes for which it was given.
> - Full and accurate accounting records are kept.
> - Taxes and business rates are paid by the organisation.
> - Tax and rate reliefs due to the organisation are collected in full.
> - The organisation is properly insured.
>
> Your MANAGEMENT responsibilities are to:
>
> - Ensure that money and assets are used efficiently and effectively to help your organisation to achieve its aims.
> - Obtain an accurate overall picture of your organisation's financial health

Accounting requirements

Accounts

If your organisation is an unincorporated, registered charity in England or Wales, you must produce accounts as prescribed by the 1992 Charities Act. If your organisation is a company limited by guarantee, you must follow the regulations of the Companies Acts. If you are registered as an Industrial and Provident Society or a Friendly Society you will have to conform to the rules of the Registrar of Friendly Societies.

The following is a summary of the accounting requirements for Charities following 1992 Charities Act (For charities in England and Wales)

All registered charities must provide the Charity Commissioners with an annual report summarising the progress of the organisation and an annual return giving basic details of the organisation, including its trustees.

They must also provide annual accounts as follows:

- If the annual income exceeds £100,000, the accounts must be professionally audited.
- If the annual income is between £25,000 and £100,000, the accounts must be examined by an independent person (unless an audit is required by their constitution).
- If the annual income is less than £25,000 simplified accounts can be provided, but these must be examined by an independent person.

Annual accounts must be made available to the public.

Unregistered charities with an annual income up to £1,000 have a duty to keep simplified annual accounts which must be available to members of the public.

Charitable companies (whatever their income) must have professionally audited accounts; provide a directors report and annual returns to both Companies House (in accordance with the Companies Acts) and the Charity Commissioners; and make their annual accounts available to the public.

All trustees should also make sure that:

- All money and assets are used solely to pursue the objects of the organisation as set out in the constitution.
- Full, accurate accounting records are kept and stored securely for at least seven years.
- Bank accounts are operated and cheques signed by more than one person.
- Cheques are not signed without details of the amount of the payment and purpose for which it will be spent.
- Funds given for different purposes are kept separate in the accounts.
- Property is under the control of the trustees.
- Tax is paid when due and tax reliefs collected in full.
- Money is not accumulated for its own sake; if you have surplus funds, you should have a specific future use in mind.
- Annual accounts are submitted to the Inland Revenue, where the charity is claiming tax reliefs.
- You register for VAT if your "taxable turnover" exceeds or will exceed the threshold level for registration; and if you are registered, that VAT returns are submitted quarterly as due.
- You keep a record of wages to satisfy Inland Revenue, PAYE and National Insurance requirements.
- Tax and National Insurance have been deducted as required before making payment to staff or for casual labour.

If your organisation is a registered charity, you should:

- Include the words charity or registered charity plus your charity registration number on headed notepaper, cheques, invoices, orders, publications, publicity material and other official documents.

If you are a director of a company limited by guarantee you must make sure that you:

- Exercise reasonable care in managing the financial affairs of the company. This is the level of care one would expect from a competent business person.
- Do not trade recklessly (for example, entering into contracts without having the assets to cover the costs).
- Include your full registered name; the words "company limited by guarantee"; your "domicile" (i.e. registered in England or Wales); and your registered office address on all headed notepaper, invoices, orders, cheques, publications and publicity material.

See *Book 4* for more detail.

Financial accountability is every trustee's affair

The trustees do not have to be accountants nor do they need to understand every detail of the accounting process. But since the trustees are together responsible for the financial health and good financial management of the organisation, it is essential that each trustee makes it their business to have a basic understanding of finance.

The more detailed financial planning and financial accounting may often be done by specialists, both amongst the trustees (the Treasurer who might be a retired bank manager, financial specialist or accountant) and by specialist members of staff (the financial director or administrator).

The Effective Trustee

TECHNICAL DETAIL

Plain talk guide to financial language

You don't need to be an accountant or to understand precisely how the accounts are compiled. You should have a sufficient understanding of the process to budget and control the organisation's finances. The following is a plain talk guide to the financial language you may encounter:

Term	Explanation
Accounts	A summary of the transactions (payments in, payments out) over a period of time. Most organisations will prepare monthly or quarterly accounts showing progress over the year, and annual accounts for each year.
Accruals	Expenses which have been incurred in an accounting period, but not yet paid (such as the phone bill which is paid in arrears).
Assets	Everything your organisation owns: money, money owed to you, equipment, property, land, stocks, investments, and so on.
Audit	A yearly report on the financial affairs of your organisation, carried out by an independent, qualified auditor. Smaller charities with an annual income of less than £100,000 do not require a full audit (unless they are established as a company limited by guarantee).
Accounting year	The twelve-month period used for your financial dealings. Organisations can choose any twelve-month period, but many have a financial year from 1st April to 31st March, which is the same as that used by local and central government.
Balance sheet	A record, of all of your organisation's assets and liabilities on a particular day (usually the last day of your financial year).
Bank reconciliation	Checking that the figures entered in your cash book match those on your bank statement.
Cash book	Details of all money received and money paid out.

Term	Explanation
Cash flow	The flow of money in and out of the organisation. Problems arise when there is not enough money in the bank to pay all your bills.
Creditors	Money owed by the organisation. (In the accounts)
Current assets	What you own or are owed, which can be readily converted into cash within one year. These include: money in the bank, stock, petty cash, money owed, and payments you have made in advance (pre-payment).
Current liabilities	The money you owe to others. This includes overdrafts, unpaid bills, grants received but not yet spent.
Debtors	Money owed to the organisation. (In the accounts)
Depreciation	The value of larger items of equipment (assets) declines each year. Depreciation is a method for showing how much the value has declined over the year. It is, in effect, the cost of using the asset. For example, a computer worth £2,000 has an expected life of 4 years. It will be depreciated by £500 each year. At the end of four years, its value will have reduced to zero.
Expenditure	Money spent to meet costs incurred by the organisation.
Fixed assets	Land, buildings, equipment, vehicles etc. have a life of more than one year. Most fixed assets will depreciate each year, but land is not depreciated (it has permanent value). Land and property should be re-valued from time ti time to reflect its value.
Income	Money coming in to the organisation.

Income and expenditure account	A yearly statement of the income and expenditure of the organisation which show all the transactions entered into during the year.	**Prepayments**	Items paid for in advance. These are treated as money owed to the organisation in the balance sheet.
		Receipts	The cheques and cash received by the organisation in return for goods or services supplied.
Net assets	The total value of all the assets less all the liabilities. This gives an indication of the net worth of the organisation.	**Receipts and payments account**	A summary of all receipts and payments in a given year. This is the simplest form of annual account. It does not reflect the true financial position of the organisation since it is only a record of the money flow. An income and expenditure account is a more accurate indicator.
Net current assets	The current assets minus current liabilities. It gives an indication of the resources available or quickly realisable, that the organisation has to hand. This is, effectively, the working capital of the organisation.		
		Signatories	People authorised to sign cheques on behalf of the organisation. At least two signatories are normally required for all payments.
Petty cash	A small (usually less than £100) sum of money taken out as cash, for day to day payment of small items. Records of payments are kept in the petty cash book.	**Solvency**	An organisation is solvent when it has sufficient assets to cover all its known liabilities (as shown on its balance sheet), or at least can pay all its bills when they fall due.
Payments	The cheques and cash payments made by the organisation. These are not necessarily made at the same time that the expenditure is incurred (see also receipts).		

Read through the terms listed above and check that you understand each one.

The components of your accounting system

- **Books of Account** recording receipt (money paid in) and payments (money paid out).
- **Files** containing invoices and receipts.
- **Stock Records** which give details of the stocks such as of publications, or other items which will be sold.
- An **Asset Register** which records details of equipment or other fixed assets.
- **Wages Records** (if staff are employed) which cover details of each person's wages, PAYE payments, national insurance payments and any other deductions.
- **Cash payments** made to individuals for work done for the organisation. There are important rules for the deduction of Income Tax and National Insurance when making these payments. It is important that these rules are meticulously observed.
- A **Covenant Register**. If you are a charity in receipt of donations by covenant, you must be able to show that covenanted payments have been made before you can re-claim tax on them.
- **Fund Accounts** which keep track of income and expenditure related to specific grants, donations or purposes.
- A **Nominal Ledger** which gathers together all the financial information from your books. The information from the nominal ledger is used to produce your annual accounts. In some organisations, the information is used to produce quarterly or monthly Trial Balances (lists of the balances in the nominal ledger). These can provide you with information about how the organisation is doing over a shorter period than the annual accounts.
- **Annual Accounts** which summarise the financial affairs over a one year period. These include your income and expenditure account and the balance sheet.
- **Management Accounts** which present your budget forecasts of money in and money spent, against actual performance during the year.

The basic principles of accounting are quite simple. Anyone who has managed their own household financial affairs with any degree of success will have some idea of the principles of forward planning, budgeting and keeping records.

You should make sure that:

- Your organisation has a proper system of accounting;
- The trustees receive sufficient information to oversee the organisation's finances effectively;
- You are able to understand the accounts and interpret the financial information you receive;
- The person who audits or inspects your accounts is happy with the way in which records are kept and accounts are produced and has given a "clean bill of health" to your latest annual accounts.

The managing committee will receive regular summaries of the financial information. Make sure you understand these. If not, ask the Treasurer, or the other trustees.

In this book we explain the basic accounting principles and some of the terms used. If you wish to find out more there are a wide range of basic accounting courses available for charity staff and trustees. You can read Book 3 which gives detailed information and worked examples of accounts.

Basic accounting systems

Your accounting system should enable you to have a picture of how the organisation is performing financially.

- Where the money being received by the organisation has come from (income accounts);
- What the money has been spent on (expenditure accounts);
- Whether the amount of money coming in is greater than or less than the amount of money being spent (surplus or deficit);
- What income and expenditure are planned for the future (budgets);
- What the assets (including cash balances and reserves) and liabilities are (the balance sheet);
- What return is being made from investments and from any money you may have sitting in a bank account (investment policy; use of cash balances);

You are expected to ensure that the organisation is getting the best reasonable return on any investments which it has, and is making the best reasonable use out of all money that has been donated.

The financial information you receive should help in your decision making. Some organisations create problems for themselves by organising their accounts so that it is very difficult to get any clear picture of how the organisation is faring.

Charities keep their accounts in different ways. Recommended accounting practice for charities is set out in a Standard of Recommended Practice - known as SORP 2 (*see Book 4*). This is recommended rather than required practice, but if your accounts have to be audited, then your auditors may expect the accounts to conform to the SORP 2 requirements.

If you are joining an organisation that already exists (rather than setting up an organisation from scratch) an accounting system will already exist. Make sure that you understand how the system works.

Information from the accounting system

Your Treasurer will summarise information from your financial records. It is the Treasurer's job to see that information is being collected and to communicate and explain this information to you.

The information you receive will come to you in two main forms: annual accounts and regular (usually monthly or quarterly) management accounts.

Annual accounts

At the end of every year your organisation must produce a statement of your finances for that year. These are your annual accounts. The responsibility for preparing these accounts usually rests with the Treasurer. Where staff are employed, the treasurer may supervise the preparation of accounts by the appropriate staff member.

The annual accounts usually consist of an income and expenditure account (which shows the flow of money in and out of the organisation for the year) and a balance sheet (which shows the assets and liabilities of the organisation at the end of the year).

Unless you are the Treasurer, you are not expected to be able to prepare these accounts. As an effective trustee you should be able to read them, understand the information they contain, and be satisfied that your organisation's financial affairs are in order. The accounts should be:

- Clear and understandable to you;
- Give you a complete picture of your financial affairs;
- Up to date and circulated in good time for you to read them;
- Comparable with the previous years' accounts, and, if possible, with the accounts of similar organisations.

The income and expenditure account

This account gives details of all transactions during the financial year. In its simplest form, the account is a record of receipts for money coming in, and

Accounts

- Since you became a trustee, have you had the accounting system explained to you?

- Do you have any questions about the system your organisation is using? Is it the most appropriate way for your organisation to handle its money? Have you raised these questions with the other trustees?

- Do you understand the accounts well enough to be confident about the information they give you?

- Is your organisation meeting its requirements to provide financial reports to others?

CHECK POINT

payments going out, in a given year. In very small organisations this may be all that is needed. This is a basic receipts and payments account.

For charities and organisations with any significant turnover, this will not be sufficient. They will need to keep an income and expenditure account. This records all transactions during the year, rather than simply the money was actually received or paid out. It is produced by making a series of adjustments to the receipts and payments account. This includes adjustment for money owed (creditors), grants and other money received in advance or not fully spent, accruals, money owed to the organisation (debtors), payments made in advance (prepayments), stock purchased and consumed, assets purchased and depreciation of assets. (See Box on page 28 for an explanation of all these terms.)

When you are presented with your organisation's income and expenditure account, you should be able to scan it quickly and identify any items on which you need more information.

Comparing the accounts to previous years

Trustees should compare the figures for income and expenditure to those of the previous year. It is usual practice to include the previous year's figures alongside. It may be valuable to look back over several years, to spot longer trends or changes.

The balance sheet

The Balance Sheet gives you a snapshot of the financial health of the organisation on the last day of the financial year.

The balance sheet summarises your organisation's assets (fixed assets and current assets) and its liabilities (the money you owe to others).
The balance sheet tells trustees whether the organisation has sufficient assets to match its liabilities, whether it has sufficient short-term assets or cash balances to meet its immediate liabilities and whether it is solvent.

> **The balance sheet** — CHECK POINT
> - Do you understand what the balance sheet tells you?
> - Are there any points where you need clarification from the Treasurer or the auditor?
> - As far as you can tell, is your organisation solvent?
> - Can you explain the balance to potential donors or supporters?

Solvency

Your organisation is solvent if its current assets exceed its current liabilities and if it has, or can obtain, sufficient cash to pay the bills when they fall due. You may not always readily be able to convert assets such as long term investments, buildings or equipment into cash or realise them at the value they appear in your balance sheet (book value), so these assets are not counted in assessing solvency.

The solvency of your organisation is of the utmost importance to trustees. If your organisation folds without sufficient assets to meet its liabilities, you may be liable to pay any shortfall out of your own pocket, if your organisation is:

- An unincorporated body (a trust or an association); or
- A company limited by guarantee and you have continued to trade when you knew that the organisation was insolvent.

Instances of trustees actually being held liable and having to make good such deficits are rare. Many organisations operate near the limits of solvency, and some unexpected occurrence can knock them over the edge - for example, a major grant not being renewed or a fundraising event going horribly wrong.

The best protection against insolvency is prudent financial management - keeping good financial control over the organisation, planning your fundraising well ahead, building good working relationship with major donors and sponsors, and possibly (if it is feasible) building or raising a reserve fund for contingencies or working capital.

If you are near or at the insolvency level, you should develop a plan for dealing with the financial crisis as quickly as you can. This may mean cutting costs, deferring expenditure and a concerted fundraising effort.

Deficit

If your organisation ends its financial year having spent more than it received, then it will have incurred a deficit for the year. If it has accumulated surpluses from previous years, then this may cover any deficit run up during the year. If it doesn't, then the organisations may have to carry forward a deficit (and may be technically insolvent). You should distinguish a short term deficit for particular identifiable reasons, from longer term, underlying, financial

Scrutinising the annual accounts

Look at your organisation's latest annual accounts.

Read the income and expenditure account.

- Check that you understand it. If not, seek clarification from the Treasurer.
- Compare it to previous years' accounts. Are there any significant changes? Check that you understand the reasons for the changes.
- What are the main changes in income? Are these trends continuing in the present year? Are the major grants secure for the immediate future? What sources of income will be terminating?
- Have any items of expenditure increased sharply over the period? If so, why? Are there any foreseeable increases in the current year, or future years?
- Is the organisation in surplus or deficit?
- What will you do with the surplus?
- What action will you take to deal with any deficit? - Find out whether the deficit is caused by short term factors. When will you cease to be in deficit? How will you reduce or resource the deficit?

Read the balance sheet

- Check you understand it. If not, seek clarification from the Treasurer or other trustees.
- Compare the balance sheet with the previous 2-3 years. Look for any trends. Is the organisation holding its own? Is it making a surplus and building up reserve funds? Is it making a deficit and using up its reserves and assets?
- Examine how your investments and other assets have performed (see Chapter 5). Are you getting a good enough return on your assets?
- Does the organisation have sufficient resources to undertake its programme of work? Will it be able to raise the resources it will need? If not, what action is required?

Does the organisation appear (a) extremely rich, with large accumulated balances or, (b) extremely stretched and nearly insolvent? If so you will need to think carefully how you present the picture of the financial state of the organisation in your accounts and to potential supporters.

Identify any changes that you think should be made in next year's budget on the basis of this year's financial performance of the organisation.

Identify any issues to feed in to your fundraising strategy *(Chapter 6).*

ACTIVITY

problems. If you have any doubts, seek a discussion with the Treasurer, or place an item on the agenda for the next managing committee meeting.

A large deficit will make it appear that you are financially incompetent. A large surplus for the year makes it appear that you are not able to use the resources you have, and this can make fundraising more difficult. In either case, you may need to attach a note to your accounts clearly explaining the situation, why it arose and what you are doing about it.

The budget

The annual budget is a financial plan for the year ahead. A long-term budget will project the income and expenditure over the next 3 or even 5 years. Budgeting is a vital part of your organisation's planning process. It provides you with a

The Effective Trustee

Types of budget

Balanced budget:
income matches expenditure

Surplus budget:
more income than expenditure (makes a profit)

Deficit budget:
more expenditure than income (makes a loss)

Charities usually budget for a balance or to achieve a small surplus. They are not supposed to accumulate large surpluses for no purpose. Most funders will be unhappy if the organisation does not spend all of the money that they provide.

TECHNICAL DETAIL

financial framework for managing and controlling your operations. It is a tool for controlling expenditure, and it gives advance notice of what income you need to raise.

Trustees should always be involved in discussing the organisation's budget before it is fully agreed. You should:

- Check that the budget reflects the priorities and plans of your organisation. Are resources being focused on the work that is most important?
- Check the assumptions underlying the main areas of income and expenditure. Will income rise as

Approaches to drawing up the budget

TECHNICAL DETAIL

The budget predicts income to be generated and the expenditure which will be incurred for the next twelve months. Predictions are made on the basis of known costs, known income, estimated costs of new activities, estimates of new income, and so on. There are three main approaches:

Incremental *"Last year's money plus a bit more."* The organisation reviews its income and expenditure for the previous year, and adds a percentage for the coming year to cover inflation, growth in activities, or increasing costs. This assumes that the original budgets were properly analysed and doesn't really explore what it will cost to carry out the priority objectives of the organisation. This method does not cope well with changes in the activities of the organisation.

Zero sum: *"What it will cost to do the work we want, in the way we want to do it."* The organisation, and each project or department within it, works out what services or activities it will carry out and what it will cost to achieve them. This involves detailed consideration of priorities and plans, as well as careful analysis of costs. It has fundraising implications, as the organisation must be able to raise the money it plans to spend. If it can't, it will have to review its spending plans.

Ad hoc: *"Tell us what you need, and we'll consider it."* A mixture of both the above methods. Some items are increased by a percentage; others are analysed for their real costs; new items may be introduced and argued for.

Resources are always limited. In each of these approaches you will need to decide upon priorities - which area of work has most need of more resources and why? Trustees play the essential role of deciding which direction the organisation should take, how to allocate existing resources and how much effort to put into generating new resources.

anticipated? Why are costs increasing in any particular area?
- See that costs are kept as low as possible, to keep your activities as efficient as possible
- Make sure that the annual budget is a part of your organisation's long term plans. For example, you may decide to operate with a deficit budget for 2 or 3 years, whilst building up your fundraising capacity.

The annual budget is often broken down in to quarterly or monthly periods, to allow the organisation to monitor closely actual performance against the budget. For further reading on budgeting see *Books 3 and 5*.

Drawing up the budget

Drawing up your budget is the responsibility of the Treasurer. The task is often delegated to a paid member of staff (such as the Director, Finance Officer, Administrator), or to a Finance Sub-Committee. It should be done well in advance of the year it covers. Many organisations have budgets that cover the financial year from April 1st to March 31st. Budgets are usually drafted in the Autumn of the previous year and confirmed a month or more before the start of the financial year.

A typical sequence would be: discuss the draft budgets in September; check details from major funders in the Autumn; confirm budgets in January; budget comes into operation on April 1st.

Cash flow

Cash flow refers to the flow of money in and out of the organisation. Where an organisation has limited cash balances, any substantial expenditure can create short-term problems of cash flow. There may not be enough money to pay the bills, even though the budget for the year, balances.

Using your budget

CHECK POINT

- Does your organisation produce a budget?
- What assumptions are made about increases in income and expenditure?
- What new income and expenditure is expected?
- What new developments are planned? Are they a priority for you? Do you have the resources to undertake them?
- Are you planning to spend your resources sensibly? Will you spend too much on work which is relatively unimportant?
- Do you have a strategy for raising the money you need? Who is responsible for the fundraising? Have outside factors (like the economy, or government spending plans) been taken into consideration?
- On what basis do you calculate the costs of wages? What increase (if any) has been allowed to cover inflation? How do you recognise increased experience and performance of members of your staff?
- Have you included the value of donations "in kind" and of volunteers' work in your calculations?
- Are you spending enough to keep staff and volunteers fully trained, so that they provide high quality work?
- Have you cut corners? Are you saving money in the short term, but storing up problems for later (for example by not keeping a building in a good state of repair)? Are you trying to provide a Rolls Royce service on a Mini budget?
- Does the budget allow room for the unexpected? Will it collapse if you have to buy one more extra paper clip or if their is a deluge on your flag day?
- Does the budget balance? If not, will this cause problems?

If an organisation is largely dependent on one grant, and that grant is paid late, cash flow problems can often result.

The Treasurer should produce a cash flow forecast for the year, as part of the budgeting process. This will tell trustees when income is expected, how much money there will be in the bank, and whether there will be sufficient to make the payments that are expected.

If the cash flow forecast shows a shortfall, the organisation may need to cover the deficit from any reserves, by selling other assets or by arranging a bank overdraft. Your budget should always include the costs of such loans or overdrafts.

Cash-flow problems are usually short-term. They should not be confused with deficits on annual income and expenditure. Cash flow is, however, extremely important. If you cannot pay your staff, or for goods or services you have purchased, you may face a financial crisis.

Management accounts

Management accounts compare the **actual** income and expenditure of the organisation with the **budgeted** figures.

The comparison is usually done each month or quarter (depending on the size of your organisation). Each item in the budget is compared to the actual figure taken from financial records. Any **variance** is noted. If the variance is significant, the reasons should be discussed. If necessary, the budget forecasts may need to be changed as a result.

Management accounts are used to monitor how the organisation is doing. They can alert you to problems of overspending or a shortfall in fundraising as they begin to develop. You are then ready to take action to remedy them. Discussing management accounts usually takes up a substantial amount of managing committee time - they may be on the agenda at each meeting.

When you discuss the management accounts you should:

- Concentrate on any significant variance between the budget and the actual figures (for both income and expenditure).

Management accounts: what to do if there are problems

Income is greater than expected.
Is it just a seasonal fluctuation? Or can you afford to plan more activities based on the new figures?

Expenditure is greater than expected.
What is the cause? Can costs be pruned back? Will this lead to operating problems?

Income is less than expected.
Is it seasonal? Is it caused by a known event? Will it be made up later in the year?

Expenditure less than expected?
Do you know why? Will it continue?

Possible action if there are difficulties

- Cut back on costs as far as possible.
- Reduce planned activities.
- Increase income from fundraising, sales, fees charges, etc.
- Expand activities if this will generate more income.
- Accept the deficit, but build a remedy into next year's plans.
- Reduce staffing levels.
- Realise assets.
- Consider the idea of winding up the organisation.

Think carefully through the best course of action.

Don't leap to hasty action - the variance may be slight, in the overall scheme of things, and may be easily remedied by better financial management over several years.

Don't try to use money given for one purpose for other purposes: this is not generally allowed. It could put the trustees in breach of trust.

Don't ignore the matter and hope that it will put itself right of its own accord.

- Make sure you understand the reason for these variances.
- Look for trends in the accounts. Has one figure been consistently out of line for several months? And if so, why?
- Reach decisions which you hope will resolve the problems.
- Adjust your annual budget according to the new decisions you have made. But make sure the budget is still viable, and that you will remain solvent.

Early in your financial year you may have too little information to be able to make accurate judgements on whether things are really going wrong. Later in the year, you will have a clearer picture, but it may be too late to put things right. For this reason, it is particularly important that the management accounts are produced regularly and scrutinised carefully by the trustees.

Restricted income or fund accounting

Some money is given to the organisation for particular a purpose. The donor specifies what it must be used for. Such money is known as restricted income. It may be accounted for separately in the organisation's accounts or by operating a separate bank account. This money should not be used for any other purpose. If you allow it to be used for any other purpose you will be in "breach of trust" and the trustees might be required, personally, to repay some or all of the money.

If too much income is restricted, the organisation may not have enough flexibility in planning its work, as it will have little money that can be used for general purposes. Most organisations try to get a sufficient amount of unrestricted income. This can be used to pursue any of the organisation's objects.

If you find that you cannot spend your income on the purpose for which it was

Cash flow and management accounts

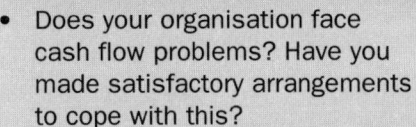

- Does your organisation have a cash flow forecast?
- Does your organisation face cash flow problems? Have you made satisfactory arrangements to cope with this?
- Does your organisation produce management accounts? How frequently? How soon after the period to which they refer, are they produced?
- Do you understand them? If not, why? Have you sought clarification from the treasurer or appropriate staff member?
- Do you play an active part in discussion of the management accounts?

CHECK POINT

given, you will either have to get the agreement of the donor to spend it on another purpose, or you will have to return it.

Delegation to a finance sub-committee

In larger organisations, detailed monthly consideration of management accounts may be delegated to a Finance Sub-Committee. The trustees are given reports on any significant matters arising from the sub-committee's work. This spares the whole governing body the task of detailed financial supervision, every month.

Smaller organisations may delegate much of this work to the Treasurer, together with the financial administrator (if such a person is employed). The Treasurer will report to each meeting of the trustees on any significant matters arising from the management accounts. The trustees may require a discussion on progress, perhaps every six months.

Remember, even where the detailed scrutiny of the management accounts is delegated, you and all the other trustees remain legally responsible for your organisation's finances.

How to respond to a financial crisis

One thing that seems to bring managing committees to life is a financial crisis.

An effective group of trustees will have taken all possible steps to avoid a crisis. They will:

- Plan well ahead.
- Set realistic budgets.
- Raise money in a thought-out way.
- Identify problems early.
- Take the necessary action in good time to prevent problems turning into a crisis.

Despite the best planning, factors outside your organisation's control may trigger a crisis. These include: loss of a large grant; a sudden unexpected expense, such as a building repair or vehicle breakdown; a dramatic downturn in donations or the failure of a fundraising appeal.

If this happens you should consider taking the following steps:

1. Immediate action:

- Recover all the money owed to the organisation.
- Delay paying bills (if you must) for as long as possible.
- Cut costs as much as possible - without bringing your services to a halt.

2. Contingency plans

- Draw up a recovery plan to get your finances and the organisation's work back on an even level.
- Talk to your major funders: is there any way they can help you through the crisis? Can they give you a special grant? If they believe in your work they may find a way to tide you over.
- If the crisis is temporary, can you negotiate a low interest or interest-free loan? If not, would a bank loan help?
- If the crisis appears long-term, can you survive by cutting back services, laying off staff and keeping a core of activity going?
- If the crisis appears terminal, plan to wind up the organisation, with minimum damage to clients, staff, volunteers and other parties.

Independent examination of your accounts

The 1992 Charities Act requires charities in England and Wales with an annual income of over £1,000 to have their accounts examined by an independent person. For larger charities, with an income of more than £100,000, a full annual audit by a qualified auditor is required. The Companies Act requires an audit for all companies limited by guarantee. Your constitution may lay down that your accounts be audited each year.

An independent examiner is defined as "a person who is reasonably believed by the trustees to have the requisite ability and practical experience to carry out a competent examination of the records." Independent examination is a similar process to an audit, but is less rigorous.
An auditor is a person who is eligible to carry out audits for charities as defined by the Secretary of State for the Home Office, or eligible under the 1989 Companies Act (this means registered auditors who must be regulated by a recognised body. Not all accountants are registered auditors).

What the auditor does

The auditor will:

- Check that all money has been spent in line with the objects of the organisation.
- Check that all money spent and due has been properly recorded and accounted for.
- Examine the record keeping systems (receipts, cheques bank statements,

etc.) and assess whether these are adequate.

- Assess whether the accounts and internal controls are sufficient.
- Verify that the annual accounts give a true and accurate picture of the financial health of the organisation.

The extent of the auditor's work will vary, depending on the nature of your organisation's activities. Make sure that you are clear what the auditor does and, equally important, does not do.

If all seems to be satisfactory the auditor will declare she or he is satisfied with the accounts and any limits to their audit. The auditor will, in most cases, be paid for their professional services.

Are you satisfied with your auditor?

The auditor should provide you with clear audited accounts, and if requested, a management letter which gives further information on the finances of the organisation (such as recommendations to eliminate weaknesses of systems, or the state of your financial affairs). You must be able to understand the audited accounts, and if necessary have them explained to the committee by the auditor.

You must be confident in your auditors professional expertise. You should also be convinced that you are getting good value for money. If not, your organisation should shop around. Ask other organisations who they use as auditors. Are they satisfied? What do they pay?

Some auditors may agree to work for reduced fees, or in an honourary capacity, donating their professional services to your charity.

Handling cash

Trustees of organisations which receive cash donations, or make cash sales, must

Examination of your accounts

- How is the auditor or independent examiner appointed? (Your constitution may set down a procedure for appointing (or re-appointing) your auditor.)
- How much are you paying in professional fees?
- Are you happy with the service you are getting?
- Have you read the audited accounts?
- Are they clear and understandable?
- Are the explanatory notes comprehensible?
- Have you asked for a management letter?
- Have you noted and dealt with any points arising from the letter?

CHECK POINT

ensure that they have proper procedures for receiving and banking this cash. Make sure you are satisfied that you have a watertight system:

- Always give receipts (using a numbered receipt book) for cash donations, unless it is impossible.
- Always record donations received.
- Keep incoming money completely separate from any cash payments you make.
- Limit access to petty cash boxes to authorised staff.
- Keep cash transactions to an absolute minimum - use cheques wherever possible.
- Always pay surplus cash into the bank.
- Have clear, safe procedures for opening collecting boxes and envelopes containing donations with two people present.

Income tax and PAYE

If your organisation employs staff, the managing committee is responsible for seeing that Income Tax and National Insurance are paid on staff salaries. The Inland Revenue sets the rules for PAYE systems (*see Book 9*). You must ensure that these are strictly observed.

If you have not deducted tax and National Insurance when making payments to people working for you (whether or not you believe them to be self-employed), the Inland Revenue can hold you responsible for the payments they believe you should have made. They will treat the sum paid out as a payment net of tax, so your organisation could face a bill amounting to over two thirds of what you have actually paid. (So, if you have paid out £100, you could be asked to pay the Inland Revenue £67.) The Inland Revenue can assess you for tax on any payment during the last six years. The following precautions will ensure that your organisation does not run the risk of an unexpected tax charge, or a prosecution:

- Operate PAYE in accordance with the Inland Revenue's rules.
- When hiring self-employed people on contracts, make sure they are registered with the Inland Revenue.
- Always get and keep invoices for work done by outside contractors.
- Keep records of payments made to contractors with their details, for six years.
- Keep a record of all casual payments made in a wages or cash book.

Avoid paying by cash. Where possible deduct Income Tax and National Insurance from casual payments, except for payments made to full-time students for vacation work, on submission of the required tax form.

Payments to volunteers

Volunteers (including trustees) may be re-imbursed for genuine expenses incurred in carrying out their work. Your organisation should have a procedure for doing this, which spells out when and how volunteers may claim expenses and for what. No tax is payable on such expenses.

Where active volunteers receive large sums in expenses there can be problems. For example, volunteer drivers are allowed to claim a tax free mileage allowance up to a maximum rate per mile, for up to a maximum number of miles travelled per year (currently 4,000). Above this limit, income tax is payable.

Volunteers who receive honoraria (small, annual payments to cover expenses incurred in their work) may be regarded as employees, and become liable for tax. You should seek a dispensation from the Inland Revenue to avoid liability for tax. If in any doubt, get advice from the Inland Revenue.

Volunteers who receive welfare benefits face restrictions on the amount of money or in-kind benefits they can receive without affecting their benefit payments. Genuine out-of-pocket expenses are not restricted, but other payments are (*as at June 1993*):

- Volunteers on unemployment benefit can receive up to £2 per day or a maximum of £54 per week.
- Volunteers on income support can receive a maximum of £5 per week.

In both these cases volunteers must continue to be available for work within 24 hours. Volunteers must also be actively seeking work and are expected to report each week on steps that have been taken to find work.

Your main responsibility as a trustee is to see that your organisation has up-to-date information on this, and has proper procedures to make sure that both your organisation and your volunteers are protected. *Book 10* gives details.

Registration for VAT

Trustees must ensure that the organisation is registered for VAT, if its annual turnover is over the threshold for doing so. Organisations registered for VAT must make accurate VAT returns, and submit them on time, or face penalties. VAT is administered by HM Customs and Excise who have wide powers to collect VAT that is due.

If the organisation makes taxable supplies of over £37,600 in any year (the VAT threshold for 1993/94), then it will be required to register for VAT. This includes sales of publications and services (except services provided at below cost) and sponsorship income. It excludes donations, fundraising and some subscription income. The rules as to what counts and what doesn't count are extremely complicated, and if you are near the threshold for registration, professional advice should be sought.

Once you are registered, you have to charge VAT (currently at 17.5%) on all standard-rated supplies you make and submit a VAT invoice to your customer. You can claim back the VAT paid on any purchases you have made.

VAT

- Are you satisfied that your organisation has received appropriate, reliable and professional advice on VAT matters?
- Should your organisation be registered?
- Are there any circumstances in the future which might require you to register?
- Are your VAT returns being submitted accurately and on time?
- Do you have proper procedures for invoicing and accounting for VAT?
- Is your VAT number displayed on invoices, and elsewhere, as appropriate?

CHECK POINT

Key points to bear in mind about VAT

- VAT generally depends on the nature of the goods and services supplied. Charities do not receive any general exemption from VAT. There are a number of quite small concessions on certain types of goods and services supplied to or by charities.

- Grants and donations made without significant benefit to the donor do not attract VAT.

- Goods or services supplied under a contract may attract VAT. If your funding is moving towards a contract basis, check the VAT implications carefully.

- Some of the most important exemptions to VAT are "welfare supplies" made by organisations "otherwise than for profit": education; training or re-training for employment; and registered under-fives provision. On exempt supplies, you do not charge VAT, on the supply. But you can't claim back the VAT paid on purchases made in respect of the supply.

- Subscriptions do not generally count towards VAT unless they give benefits other than, for example, a vote at the AGM or receipt of the annual report.

- Registering for VAT means you charge VAT on appropriate goods and services. You do not lose any money, but you are responsible for collecting the VAT, which can be time-consuming. An advantage of being VAT registered is that your organisation can reclaim VAT it has paid on its purchases.

- If your organisation should have registered for VAT, but didn't, it is liable to pay all the VAT owed from the moment it became liable for it. There are severe penalties for non-registration. If the organisation does not have the resources to pay this, then trustees might face personal liability. So, make sure you have a sound advice on your VAT liabilities.

If in any doubt, seek advice from your own professional advisers (accountant or auditor) or from your local Customs and Excise Branch *(see phone book).*

VAT is extremely complicated. It is essential that you are given proper, professional advice on VAT by your accountant or auditor. Various free leaflets are available from the local VAT office (*see Book 8*). An up-to-date, detailed summary of VAT as it affects voluntary organisations is available in *Book 5*.

Insurance

The trustees must see that the organisation is properly insured. Insurance gives your organisation protection against claims arising as a result of its activities, or from events which might affect it. Some insurance cover is compulsory:

- Employer's liability insurance covers claims by employees for injury or disease arising from their work. This does not usually cover voluntary workers.
- Public liability insurance covers claims for injury or damage to members of the public as a result of negligence on the part of the organisation. You should check that your policy covers your voluntary workers (including the trustees!).
- Buildings insurance covers repairs to, or replacement of buildings. It is required when you lease, or take out a mortgage, on a building. Check that you have adequate insurance on any buildings your organisation owns.
- Vehicle insurance must cover the drivers of vehicles your organisation owns against claims arising from third parties.

Your organisation may face other risks, depending on its activities. You should take out insurance to cover any reasonable risks you can foresee, such as:

- Trustee indemnity insurance protects trustees against certain personal liabilities that can arise as a result of their trusteeship. *(See "The Effective Trustee: Part One)*
- Contents insurance covers the contents of your buildings against theft or damage. This can be extended to include equipment used outside the building.
- Professional indemnity insurance protects against claims arising from negligent or incorrect advice given by the organisation.
- Vehicle insurance to cover repair or replacement of damaged vehicles.

The trustees should make sure that the organisation has assessed the risks of claims being made against it and has secured insurance protection against a reasonable level of risk. If in any doubt, you should seek professional advice, or consult a suitable insurance broker.

Self-assessment

Accounting for your organisation

	Know	Must check
1. What are the main legal requirements for the way your organisation keeps and reports on its accounts?	☐	☐
2. Do you understand the main terms used in financial management?	☐	☐
3. Who carries responsibility for the financial health of your organisation?	☐	☐
4. What do you need to have a basic picture of your organisation's financial performance?	☐	☐
5. What are the annual accounts?	☐	☐
6. What assumptions does your organisation use when drawing up its annual budget?	☐	☐
7. What are management accounts and how should trustees use them?	☐	☐
8. What steps should trustees take in the event of a financial crisis?	☐	☐
9. What is the role of the auditor or independent examiner of your accounts?	☐	☐
10. What insurance cover is compulsory for most organisations?	☐	☐

Chapter 5

Managing your finances

> **Your responsibilities**
>
> The managing committee has general responsibility for looking after the assets of the organisation.
>
> Your TRUSTEE responsibilities are:
>
> *NEED TO KNOW*
>
> - To keep property under the control of the Trustees.
> - To use any land or buildings for the charity's purposes or to let it for the maximum possible return.
> - To ensure buildings are maintained in good condition and are properly insured.
> - To make investments as authorised in your constitution, or under the Trustees Investments Act 1961.
> - To monitor the performance of investments, avoiding speculation and ensuring both income and capital growth.
> - To obtain professional advice about your investment policy.
>
> You must ensure that all the assets of the organisation are used entirely to promote its objects, and to the advantage of your beneficiaries.
>
> Your MANAGEMENT responsibility is to ensure that the organisation has proper systems and procedures for looking after its assets effectively. To fulfil this responsibility you need to know:
>
> - What assets your organisation has;
> - The investment powers given to the organisation in its governing instrument;
> - How to maintain and manage all your assets effectively.

What are assets?

The assets of your organisation fall under five headings:

- Equipment
  including office equipment, vehicles, equipment used by the organisation in its work.
- Property
  buildings and land owned or leased by the organisation for its own use.
  building and land held as an investment.
- Stock
  stocks of items produced by the organisation for sale.
- Cash
  balances in bank and building society accounts.
- Investments
  money invested long-term in shares, bonds and fixed interest securities.

Equipment

You must make sure that all your organisation's equipment is being properly recorded. This asset register should list all your equipment, giving details of date of purchase, supplier, cost of purchase, warranties and details of maintenance.

Equipment should be properly serviced and maintained. You should see that, where appropriate, people using equipment are properly trained and that all relevant health and safety regulations are enforced.

Equipment should be insured, so that it can be replaced in the event of loss or damage. You should ensure that the policy covers the use of the equipment by staff and volunteers.

Every piece of equipment has a life span. The value of the equipment should be depreciated in the accounts. This reflects the cost of using the equipment, and allows money to be set aside for its replacement at the end of its useful life.

Donated equipment or equipment purchased at a discount is treated in the same way. Its real value is depreciated. The accounts should reflect the cost of replacing the item, when calculating its depreciation.

Equipment that stands idle is a wasted asset. Make sure you are getting the maximum use out of all the equipment you own. If you hire it out to generate an income, make sure to your organisation charges enough to cover all insurance, administration, and a proportion of the replacement costs.

Property

Your organisation's property can be considered in two parts: the buildings and land you occupy for your charitable work, whether these are leased or owned; and any property you hold for investment purposes.

If your organisation has land or buildings held as investment, you should make sure that it is properly maintained and insured. You should also:

- See that you get the best possible return from renting property;
- Make sure your property is re-valued from time to time, to reflect its current value in your accounts.

Looking after the property you occupy

The managing committee should make sure that premises are properly looked after in the following ways:

- If you don't own the freehold of the property you occupy, check the terms of your lease. Note the points at which the rent is reviewed and your renewal rights when the lease terminates.
- Check your obligations under the lease for repairs and other matters. Make sure you don't take on obligations which you cannot afford.
- See that your premises are well maintained and that sufficient reserves are being set aside each year to cover the cost of redecoration or refurbishment.
- Make sure that all health and safety requirements are met.
- Check that your premises are fully insured.
- Check that buildings are being occupied and space used to best effect.
- Make sure that the premises are adequate to meet the present and future needs of your work. If not, start looking for extension or replacement premises
- Visit the premises from time to time to get a feel for them. What sort of condition are they in? What is the atmosphere like? Such things as a loose slate, or damaged gutter or a damp patch can alert you to the fact that the property is not being properly maintained.
- Make sure you are claiming the full relief on rates. (80% if your organisation is a charity, with a further 20% relief available at the discretion of the local rating authority.)

Premises and equipment are a window on your organisation

▶ **Many people will see only your premises, vehicles or other equipment. You should make sure that these convey a good impression of your organisation. Shabby, down-at-heel premises may not help either your image or staff morale. Out-of-date machinery or office equipment may limit your effectiveness. Old vehicles may be less comfortable, less safe and ultimately more expensive than newer ones.**

PRACTICAL POINTER

The Effective Trustee

Equipment and Property

CHECK POINT

- Is your equipment up-to-date and effective?
- Is your equipment properly maintained and serviced?
- Is equipment depreciated each year?
- Are funds being set aside to replace equipment?
- Is your equipment properly insured?
- Are staff trained to use equipment safely?
- Are you satisfied that your premises and buildings are being properly managed and maintained?
- Do your premises give the right atmosphere and reflect the image of the organisation?
- How often do you review the state of your equipment and buildings?

Who holds your investment property?

If your organisation is incorporated, the organisation can hold its property directly, in its own name. If it is not (if it is a trust or an association), its property must be held by named (holding) trustees. One consequence of this is that the property must be transferred to new holding trustees on the retirement or death of the existing ones. This can add to the expense of running the charity. One solution is to incorporate your trustees under the 1872 Incorporation of Trustees Act. Another is to make use of the services of the Official Custodian, who can hold land and buildings on behalf of charities.

Stock

If your organisation keeps stocks of goods for sale, such as publications, the managing committee must make sure that:

- There is a system for keeping records of stock, so that it is all accounted for.
- It is safely and securely stored. Make sure that fire regulations have been met.
- It is fully insured.
- The quantity of stock is in line with the amount your organisation expects to sell. How many years' stock will you keep? Is some stock out of date? Should it be disposed of?
- You should keep an accurate record of stock values. Stock that you don't expect to sell should be written off or written down in value in your accounts.

Cash

You and the other trustees should ensure that any cash your organisation holds is earning the maximum in interest. You need to:

- Be aware where cash is held and in what sort of accounts (current, bank deposit, building society), of the levels of interest being received on balances and any account charges levied.
- Have a system to move cash balances to interest bearing accounts as quickly as possible. Money should not be left on current account, where it earns you nothing.
- Make sure you have access to money placed in high-yielding accounts when you are likely to need it.
- Be cautious of accounts offering well above market rates of interest. In the wake of Bank of Credit and Commerce International collapse, trustees are reminded to be prudent with all investments and not put all their eggs in one basket if there is any significant degree of risk.

If your organisation has large cash balances, you should explore all the options to achieve the best return on your money. These include the money market and high interest business reserve accounts operated by any bank. There are two schemes which cater specifically for charities:

- Charities Aid Foundation - CAFcash, which is a money deposit scheme run by the Charities Aid Foundation.

- The Charities Deposit Fund run by the Charities Official Investment Fund (COIF).

See Chapter 7 for the addresses of these two schemes.

Investments

Investment powers and responsibilities

Read the governing instrument of your organisation. It will usually contain clauses which define the investment powers available to the trustees. Where no such powers are given in the governing instrument, you will be subject to the requirements of the 1961 Trustee Investments Act. It is important that you do not stray outside these powers.

If your organisation is a charity, you have certain legal responsibilities regarding investments. Trustees are expected to exercise care and prudence in managing the investments of the organisation, but not to be so cautious as to fail to get a reasonable rate of return. All investments involve some level of risk. As a trustee you should make sure that the investments:

- Are reasonably diversified to avoid unnecessary risk;
- Achieve the best, reasonable returns, in the interests of the charity;
- take in to account present and future needs, don't become too focused on short term returns;
- Do not risk the capital of the investment funds for the sake of higher returns;
- Are regularly reviewed.

When making investment decisions or reviewing your portfolio of investments, you must take investment advice from a person you believe qualified to give such advice. This could be an investment adviser, accountant or bank manager.

> **Check your assets**
>
> Below is a list of some of the assets which your organisation could own. Check what your organisation actually owns. Make sure you understand how each is managed and accounted for.
>
> ☐ Cash in bank
> ☐ Stocks of goods
> ☐ Buildings you own
> ☐ Buildings you lease
> ☐ Land and buildings held as an investment
> ☐ Equipment
> ☐ Vehicles
> ☐ Cash balances
> ☐ Stocks and shares

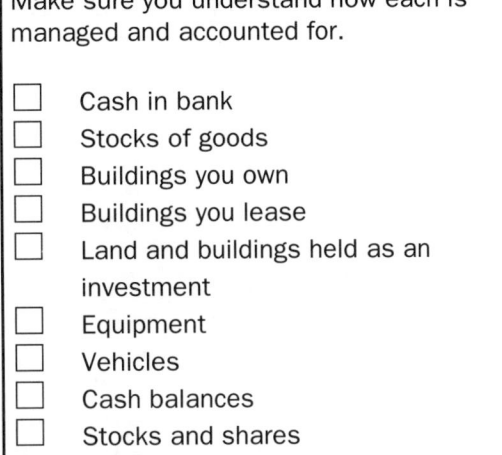

ACTIVITY

Advice should be given in writing. If it is given orally, it should all frequently be confirmed in writing.

You do not need to take advice when placing cash balances on deposit.

The Official Custodian

The Official Custodian used to hold (but not manage) investments, on behalf of charities. Under the 1992 Charities Act, all such investments are being returned to the trustees of the charities concerned. If your charity has investments that were previously held by the Official Custodian, the trustees should prepare themselves to take over their administration.

Delegation of investment

Many trustees will find that their organisation delegates its investment management to a sub-committee. Larger organisations will employ professional investment advisers or managers to assist them. Trustees should note that they can delegate the day-to-day management but they cannot delegate the responsibility for seeing that the investments are being properly managed.

> **CHECK POINT**
>
> **Stock, cash and investment**
>
> - Are you getting the best possible interest from your cash balances?
> - Is your stock properly recorded and safely stored?
> - Are you carrying the right amount of stock?
> - Have you checked your organisation's investment powers in your governing instrument?
> - Do you have an appropriate adviser for your investments?
> - Does your organisation have an investment strategy and investment policy?
> - Are you satisfied that you are getting a reasonable return on your investments?
> - Are you exposed to any unreasonable risk?
> - When were your investment performance and your investments last reviewed?

Trustees should be sure that:
- The investments are being properly managed with investment objectives which set the level of income as well as protecting the capital value of the investments.
- Investment performance is satisfactory.
- The basis on which fees are paid for investment advice is reasonable.

This should be done through regular reports and an annual review of performance. For very large portfolios, the WM Company offers assessment of the performance of the investments managed (*see Chapter 7*).

Ethical investment

Some charities require that certain areas of investment be avoided for ethical reasons. Where trustees believe that such restrictive investment policies are in the interests of the charity, then this is permitted (*see Book 15*). It may be that certain categories of investment run counter to the charity's own objectives, or because investing in a certain manner will lose the support of donors and funders. Apart from this, trustees must ensure that investment policy aims to achieve the maximum reasonable return for the charity.

Self-assessment

Managing your assets

		Know	Must check
1.	What are the five main types of assets?	☐	☐
2.	What steps should you take to see that equipment is properly managed?	☐	☐
3.	What do you need to do to make sure that the buildings you occupy are properly looked after?	☐	☐
4.	What can your organisation do to make sure it gets the best out of any positive cash balances?	☐	☐
5.	What powers do trustees have to make investments?	☐	☐
6.	What steps should trustees take to ensure sound investment management?	☐	☐

Chapter 6

Fundraising

> **⚠ NEED TO KNOW**
>
> **Your responsibilities**
>
> The managing committee is responsible for making sure that the organisation obtains sufficient money to remain solvent, and to maintain and develop its work.
>
> Your TRUSTEE responsibilities are to ensure that:
>
> - Fundraising is undertaken properly.
> - Your organisation describes the purpose of your appeals for funds accurately;
> - Your organisation is open and honest about its fundraising costs;
> - You do not use fundraising methods which exert undue pressure on people to give;
> - All legal requirements for raising money (Charities Act, Lottery Act) are met;
> - Money raised is properly accounted for;
> - The trustees approve, in advance, the fundraising methods and appeal literature that will be used;
> - Your organisation draws up a proper contract, if using professional fundraisers.
>
> Your MANAGEMENT responsibilities for fundraising are to:
>
> - Ensure your organisation has an accurate budget, so you know how much money you will need to raise now and in the future.
> - Ensure that the organisation has a sensible strategy for fundraising, so that it can maintain and develop activities. This requires you to identify those areas of fundraising which you are best able to develop and exploit
> - See that the necessary resources are provided to make the fundraising a success (time, expertise, people, promotional materials, administration).
> - Review progress on fundraising, to see that targets are being achieved, and to monitor the costs of fundraising that are incurred.
>
> Some trustees also decide to get involved as volunteers, by organising fundraising activities or asking for money. This active involvement in fundraising itself is not a requirement for trusteeship, but can make all the difference.

Fundraising and appeals committees

Your organisation may delegate the job of fundraising to a fundraising committee, a development committee, or a special appeals committee. The members of the committees do not all need to be trustees. The committee should report back to the overall managing committee on a regular basis.

The task of a fundraising committee will be to draw up a fundraising plan (*see below*) year by year, and to take active steps to see that it is carried out. This may involve:

- Delegating some of the fundraising to staff (such as writing grant applications);
- Bringing people with good contacts on to the committee, who can help ask for money;

- Employing a fundraiser as part of the organisation's staff or engaging a professional fundraiser;
- Setting up other committees or working groups to pursue particular aspects of fundraising (such as a legacy sub-group, or an events committee);
- Setting up an Appeal Committee, where the organisation intends to run a large scale one-off appeal for funds, often to mark an anniversary or a move to new premises.

Your fundraising committee should be made up of people who are committed to raising the money, who like doing it and who have the skills to do it. This committee must work well. Overall responsibility for seeing that the organisation has sufficient funds and that it is taking reasonable steps to acquire them still lies with the managing committee.

If your organisation has no fundraising committee, then the whole task of managing the fundraising falls to the managing committee. If there are no paid staff either, then all the fundraising work has to be carried out by the committee or by volunteers.

Your fundraising plan

Your organisation may need funds to:
- Continue existing activities and services and to fund the running of the organisation;
- Purchase equipment;
- Provide future security (by building up reserves or an endowment);
- Enable future development or expansion;
- Develop special projects and new activities this year and in future years.

Your organisation's strategic plan will identify the main new developments over the next one to three years. Each of these can be costed, and fundraising targets set. Your annual budget will tell trustees what income is required to keep the existing activities going for the coming year. This gives you the basis for your annual fundraising targets. Much of the fundraising here may be regular and ongoing. These two sets of targets (regular and new developments) form the starting point for your fundraising plan. The plan should set out:

- What you need to raise (budgets);
- Why you need it (purpose and priorities);
- Who you will approach for funds;
- How you will make the approach;
- What methods you will use;
- Who will be responsible for doing it or seeing it is done;
- What resources they will need to do the job effectively;
- When each stage of the fundraising process will take place;
- Contingency plans should you fail to reach your targets;
- How you will judge success.

Book 18 provides more detail.

A strategic approach to fundraising

You should try to think strategically about your fundraising. The main points to consider are:

- Who are your supporters now?
- Are you getting all the support you should expect from statutory (official) sources?
- What are the interests and concerns of your supporters? Why do they support you? Is this support likely to change?
- Which people or funding bodies do you plan to attract as supporters in future?
- How will you attract these new supporters? What are their interests and concerns?

The Effective Trustee

TECHNICAL DETAIL

Fundraising methods

Organisations use a wide variety of methods to raise funds. The list below is a brief summary of the main possibilities. *See Books 18, and 21 for more detail.*

1 Membership and supporters

The members of your organisation pay an annual subscription. This provides a regular income.

You may have a list of supporters who have given money and may give again if asked. Some of these may give regularly by Deed of Covenant or standing order.

2 General Public

Personal contacts:
Volunteers meet potential donors who are known to them and ask for money. Personal contacts can be used to reach quite large numbers of people - e.g. each volunteer collects money from ten people.

Street collections:
Volunteers collect money in sealed boxes, on the street or in public places. You will normally need to get a licence from your local authority.

House to house collections:
Volunteers collect money through door-to-door collections. This also requires a permit.

Static collections:
Use of collecting boxes in pubs, clubs or shops.

Adverts:
Placing advertisements in the local and national press, or on television.

Posters:
Use of posters and bill boards to reach a wide audience.

Publicity:
Getting editorial or news coverage of your work in the local or national press.

Leaflets:
The distribution of fundraising leaflets door-to-door, in public places, shops, and libraries.

Events:
There is an enormous number of events which can be used to raise money: fetes; carnivals; fairs; concerts; quiz nights; sponsored activities; treasure hunts - only your imagination will limit you *(see book 19)*.

Radio and television appeals:
Radio and television can be used both locally and nationally to appeal for support.

Direct mail:
This involves sending a carefully worded appeal letter to a very large number of households. The mailings can be targeted at particular areas, or social groups.

Gambling:
You can use lotteries, raffles and competitions to raise money. Their conduct is governed by rules and guidelines which should be strictly observed *(see book 18)*.

3 Legacies

Many people leave money to charity in their wills. Many solicitors ask about charitable bequests when helping a client to draw up a will. A well managed strategy to attract legacies can yield a lot of money.

4 Trading

The selling of goods or services can generate money for your organisation. Many charities make a charge for the services they offer. Some sell goods made by the beneficiaries of the charity (such as in sheltered workshops). Christmas cards, promotional items and the sale of donated goods are other common methods. The legal and tax requirements for charity trading are extremely complicated. If the activity is substantial, regular or generating a significant level of profit, you may need to seek professional advice.

5 Corporate Donations

Support from companies can be in cash, in kind, or through staff time, provision of expertise or employee volunteering. Many companies have a budget for gifts to charity *(see Book 22)*.

Sponsorship involves an agreement between your organisation and a sponsor, in which both parties benefit. You hope to raise funds, the sponsor hopes to gain publicity, or obtain some other benefit. Sponsorship of this type may be considered a trading activity and potentially liable for VAT. So, if you are offering anything more than just recognition of the donation, make sure you consult your legal and financial advisers.

6 Grant making trusts

These divide into local charitable trusts which give money to local causes. You may have to do local homework to identify these. And national charitable trusts which give money to organisations across the country.

Charitable trusts exist to donate money to charity. Each has its own procedures and priorities. You should first find out which charities support the kind of project for which you are seeking funds. Find out details about each of these trusts from directories, such as *Books 23 and 24*. These are usually available in public libraries.

Once you have established that a trust might be able to support your project, you should find out how to apply, either from the directory or by contacting the trust for further information.

7 Government

Local authorities are a major source of income for voluntary organisations. You usually apply to the relevant department. Each has procedures for making grants or entering into contracts for services.

Central government departments and agencies make a wide range of grants to many national organisations and to projects of national importance or significance *(see Book 25)*.

District health authorities act much like local authorities in making grants or entering into contracts for work they wish to support. The same applies to NHS trusts.

The EC makes grants for a variety of projects. The procedures for application are complex *(see book 26)*.

Fundraising methods

Read through the list of fundraising options above. Which are you using? How much of your annual budget are you raising from each? How might your organisation get more from your existing sources? What other ways could you use to raise money? Get all the trustees to complete the exercise. Discuss your thoughts. Use your discussion to review the fundraising options for your organisation, and to develop a strategy.

- Do you make an effective case for your organisation to all your potential supporters? How do they see you?
- What opportunities do you see for raising funds in the next year or so?
- Do your values or policies make it difficult to attract support from some quarters?
- Can you change your message, without compromising your values and policies to gain new supporters?
- What changes are expected in the field your organisation works in? Will there be competition from other agencies?
- Are your major sources of funding secure? If not, when will they run out? How will you replace them?
- Can you map out a strategy for fundraising over the next three to five years, which will take account of the above factors?
- What action do you need to take now, to ensure that you are ready and able to attract funds in the future?
- What skills and resources do you have in your organisation which could be mobilised successfully to raise money?

How to ask for money

You must believe in the work of your organisation, and understand why it needs money. Your task in fundraising is to be able to persuade other people to support your cause. The golden rules are:

- Present a clear, simple and persuasive case. You must be able to convince potential donors that your organisation and its work are worth

The Effective Trustee

> **Some DO's and DON'Ts when asking for money**
>
> **DO.....**
>
> - Think well ahead.
> - Be committed to your project.
> - Know what you hope to achieve.
> - Select your audience(s).
> - Tailor each approach to the person you are approaching.
> - Ask for an appropriate amounts.
> - Make maximum use of personal contacts.
> - Prepare an accurate realistic budget.
> - Be brief, specific and clear.
> - Be persistent.
> - Set deadlines and targets.
> - Thank donors and cultivate their goodwill.
> - Go back and ask for further support next year, or when you need it.
>
> **DON'T.....**
>
> - Send a duplicated mailshot to everyone.
> - Ask potentially big donors for too small an amount - it's difficult to go back for more.
> - Appeal for funds to cover your deficit.
> - Beg, be aggressive or rude.

supporting. Assume they know little or nothing about you.

- Ensure you have an accurate, detailed budget, identifying the amount you need to raise and how will be spent.
- Identify who you are addressing: different types of donor require different approaches. It is vital to find out where the interests of your donors lie, and to ensure that you focus on those aspects of your work which coincide with their interests.
- Make sure you have a fundraising plan and that what you are asking for fits logically within it.
- Ensure that you have suitable leadership for your fundraising activities. You need people who are committed and who know the right people or organisations to contact.

Whoever you are approaching, you will need to have a basic "case statement".

This should include:

- A description of your organisation.
- A description of the need or problem you are trying to tackle.
- Information on your past achievements in tackling the need.
- Evidence that your activities will make a real difference to the need.
- A brief summary of your organisation's financial situation, and details of the cost of the projects for which you are seeking money.
- Your organisation's latest annual report and accounts.

Depending on who you are approaching, you will need to modify the case statement to fit as closely as possible to the donor's particular interests.

For example, if a charitable trust gives money only to innovative projects, you should emphasise the innovative aspects of your project. Or, if a corporate donor is interested in the extent of your community involvement, you can point to your membership and its high level of commitment through volunteering.

Many donors are concerned about what will happen when their gift has been spent. Make sure your case includes some thoughts on the long-term funding of your work.

Fundraising is much simpler when an organisation has a clear direction, a positive case statement, knows the targets it wants to achieve and has prepared accurate budgets. It is no longer enough to seek support solely on the basis that your cause seems a good idea. You must ensure that anyone making a fundraising approach represents your organisation fairly and truthfully.

Who should ask for money?

Your fundraising plan should include details of who will do the work of asking

> **Legal aspects of fund-raising**
>
> - The laws covering theft, embezzlement, fraud and so on, apply to fundraising.
> - The 1992 Charities Act regulates fundraising activities carried out by anyone other than charity's own staff or volunteers paid less than £5 per week or £500 per year. It applies mainly to professional fundraisers who, in future, must:
>   - have a written contract
>   - identify the charity for which they are working
>   - state the method by which they are to be paid
>   - state how the money will be distributed (if they are earning money for more than one organisation).
> - All public collections require a permit from the local authority or an exemption order from the Charity Commissioners (where the charity collects throughout England and Wales).
> - The Lotteries Act regulates lotteries, raffles and tombolas. Small private lotteries do not require a permit, but must conform to detailed regulations. Large public lotteries must be registered with the local authority.

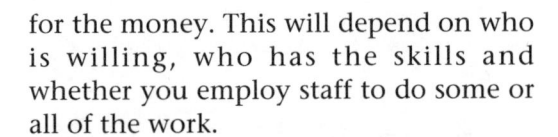

TECHNICAL DETAIL

for the money. This will depend on who is willing, who has the skills and whether you employ staff to do some or all of the work.

If you employ staff, you may expect them to do most of the leg-work for fundraising. However, trustees often play a very active part, particularly in making direct approaches to individuals, companies or trusts.

You may decide to make use of professional fundraisers. Before you proceed you should decide exactly what you want them to do and get advice from other organisations that have used professional fundraisers or from the Institute of Charity Fundraising Managers (ICFM) *(see chapter 7)*.

If you do use a professional fundraiser make sure you:

- Have a written contract.
- Have clear agreements on fees, expenses, VAT and the other costs you will be liable for.
- Agree what methods will be used and how they your organisation will be presented to potential donors.
- Agree procedures for managing the fundraising.
- Ensure that the activities comply with the law.

Some fundraisers may wish to work on a percentage basis, taking a proportion of what they raise as a fee. If they raise nothing, you pay nothing. This may appear attractive, but is generally regarded as poor practice. The 1992 Charities Act requires fundraisers to inform the donor how they will be paid. Many donors find the idea of a percentage going to the fundraiser off-putting. It is generally better to pay a proper fee and to employ professional fundraisers that you have complete confidence in.

Note that if you pay a volunteer an honorarium or a fee for their fundraising work (more than £5 per day or £500 per year), this may mean that they be classed as a professional fundraiser and that they will need to conform to the requirements of the Charities Act.

Personal contacts matter in fundraising. Your fundraising committee should do its utmost to develop and use personal contracts with potential donors. Patrons, presidents and vice-presidents may be able to play a valuable role.

Above all, you should see that fundraising approaches are planned and co-ordinated. They should be fitted in to an annual schedule, with regular reporting back to the trustees or managing committee.

Tax effective giving

If your organisation is a charity, it can benefit significantly from tax relief on donations made by tax-paying individuals or companies.

Many charities fail to take advantage of this and are losing potential income every year (see *Book 16*). Charities are entitled to recover income tax at the basic rate on all donations they receive from a donor who is a taxpayer if the money is paid by Deed of Covenant or Gift Aid.

CHECK POINT

Fundraising

- What does your managing committee do to ensure fundraising is carried out properly?
- Do you delegate the fundraising task to a fundraising or appeals committee?
- Do the trustees receive regular reports from the committee?
- Have you seen your organisation's fundraising plans?
- Are the plans coherent and in line with the organisation's overall strategy? Does your organisation present a clear, persuasive case for itself and its development, in any fundraising material you produce?
- Do your trustees approve, in advance, the fundraising methods and literature to be used?
- Are you happy with the messages and images used in your fundraising materials?
- Does your managing committee discuss your long term fundraising strategy on a regular basis? When? What form does the discussion take?

CHECK POINT

Tax effective giving

- Do you understand the benefits of tax effective giving?
- Is your charity taking full advantage of tax-effective giving? If not, what steps will you take to do so?

Deeds of covenant

For an individual who pays basic rate income tax (25%):

Annual Payment	Tax recoverable by charity	Annual Gross value
£ 7.50	£ 2.50	£ 10.00
£ 10.00	£ 3.33	£ 13.33
£100.00	£33.34	£133.34

Higher rate tax payers (paying tax at 40%) can benefit from the Higher Rate Relief, which effectively reduces the cost, to them, of their donation by 20%

A deed of covenant is a legal undertaking which binds the donor to make periodic payments from her/his income to the charity. The deed is made in writing, using a standard form of words. The covenant must run for at least four years.

Once the deed is signed, the charity is able to recover from the Inland Revenue the income tax paid on the donations made each year under the terms of the deed.

A company as well as an individual donor can enter into a deed of covenant with a charity.

Gift Aid donations

If a person or company wishes to make a once-only payment to a charity, of £250 or more, the Gift Aid scheme enables the charity to recover income tax paid. The donor must provide the charity with a certificate that the donation has been paid out of taxed income.

The tax benefits are the same as for a covenant. A £250 Gift Aid donation would be actually worth £333 to the charity and would cost a higher rate taxpayer only £200.

For details of Gift Aid *see Book 17*.
Recovering Income Tax from deeds of covenant or Gift Aid requires that proper procedures be followed precisely. If in doubt seek advice from the Inland Revenue. Tax benefits are the same as for a covenant. The Charities Aid Foundation operates a Covenant administration service for charities (*see Chapter 7*).

TECHNICAL DETAIL

Self-assessment

Fundraising

	Know	Must check
1. What should trustees do to ensure that fundraising is effective?	☐	☐
2. What are the advantages of having a fundraising committee?	☐	☐
3. What are the most common fundraising needs in a voluntary organisation?	☐	☐
4. What are the main elements of a strategic fundraising plan?	☐	☐
5. Can you list ten different fundraising methods? Which are most effective in your organisation?	☐	☐
6. What are the golden rules when asking for money?	☐	☐
7. How does the 1992 Charities Act affect professional fundraisers?	☐	☐
8. What is Gift Aid?	☐	☐
9. What is a Deed of Covenant?	☐	☐
10. Is your organisation taking full advantage of tax effective giving?	☐	☐

Chapter 7

Resources

Useful Publications

The books listed below are available from the publisher, unless otherwise stated. The publisher's address is also listed or is given in the list of useful addresses, which follows.

Planning

Book 1. Just about Managing? Effective Management for Voluntary Organisations and Community Groups. Sandy Adirondack. 1992. £10.95. London Voluntary Service Council, 68 Chalton Street, London, NW1 1JR.

Book 2. Planning Together. The Art of Effective Teamwork. George Gawlinski and Lois Graessle. Bedford Square Press. 1988. £11.95. From the National Council for Voluntary Organisations, Regent's Wharf, All Saints Street, London, N1 9RL.

Financial Management

Book 3. Accounting and Financial Management for Charities. Hilary Blume and Michael Norton. Second Edition, 1985. £7.95. Directory of Social Change, Radius Works, Back Lane, London, NW3 1HL.

Book 4. Tolley's Charities Manual. Tolley. 1991 (Updated). £65. From Tolley Publishing Company Ltd., Tolley House, 2 Addiscombe Road, Croydon, CR9 5AF.

Book 5. A Practical Guide to VAT for Charities. Kate Sayer. Directory of Social Change. 1992. £9.95. (Address above.)

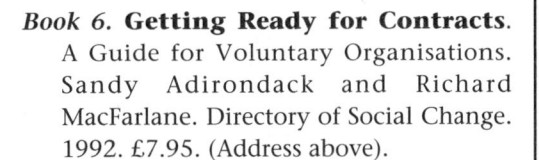

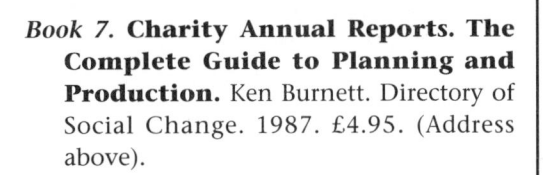

Book 6. Getting Ready for Contracts. A Guide for Voluntary Organisations. Sandy Adirondack and Richard MacFarlane. Directory of Social Change. 1992. £7.95. (Address above).

Book 7. Charity Annual Reports. The Complete Guide to Planning and Production. Ken Burnett. Directory of Social Change. 1987. £4.95. (Address above).

Book 8. Leaflets on VAT. Free from HM Customs and Excise (your local office).

700   The VAT Guide
700/1   Charities
700/5   Clubs and Associations

Book 9. Inland Revenue leaflets. Free from the Inland Revenue. (Contact your local tax office.)

P8 (1991)
Employers Basic Guide to PAYE

P7 (1991)
Employers Further Guide to PAYE

480 (1992)
Guide to expenses payments and benefits for Directors and certain employees.

Charity tax pack. Free from the Inland Revenue Claims Branch, St. John's House, Merton Road, Bootle, Merseyside, L69 9BB.

Book 10. Voluntary and part-time workers. Your benefits, pensions and National Insurance contributions. 1991. Leaflet FB 26. Free from the Social Security Agency (local office).

BOOKLIST

Evaluation

Book 11. **Working Effectively.** NCVO Practical Guide to Evaluation. Warren Feek. 1988. Bedford Square Press. From NCVO (address above). £4.95.

Book 12. **Questions of Value.** Law Centres Federation. 1988. From The Law Centres Federation, Duchess House, 18 Warren St., London W1P 5DB. £6 - £12.

Book 13. **Quality of Service. Measuring Performance for Voluntary Organisations.** Alan Lawrie. 1992. NCVO/Directory of Social Change (address above). £8.95.

Assets

Book 14. **Investment of charity funds.** John Harrison. 1993. Directory of Social Change. £7.95. (Address above).

Book 15. **Socially Responsible Investment.** Sue Ward. 1991. Directory of Social Change. £7.95. (As above).

Fundraising

Book 16. **Tax Effective Giving.** A Practical Guide. Michael Norton. 1992 (6th edition). £9.95. (Address above).

Book 17. **A Guide to Gift Aid.** Michael Norton. 1992 (2nd edition). Directory of Social Change. £7.95. (Address above).

Book 18. **The Complete Fundraising Handbook.** Sam Clarke. Second edition 1993. Directory of Social Change. £9.95. (Address above).

Book 19. **Organising Local Events.** Sarah Passingham. 1993. Directory of Social Change. £7.95. (Address above).

Book 20. **Writing better fundraising applications.** A practical guide with worked examples, exercises and ideas for workshops. Michael Norton. 1992. Directory of Social Change. £9.95. (Address above).

Book 21. **Fundraising leaflets**. Set of twelve leaflets: Setting Up; Planning a Capital Project; Drawing up a Budget; Raising Money Locally; Earning Money; Organising an Appeal; Doing Research; Writing an Application; Social Sponsorship; Developing a Strategy; Organising an Event; Fundraising Sources. Directory of Social Change. £7.50. (Address above).

Book 22. **A Guide to Company Giving.** Ed. Michael Eastwood. Directory of Social Change. 1993. £14.95. (Address above.)

Book 23. **The Directory of Grant Making Trusts.** 1993 edition. £50.00. Charities Aid Foundation, 48 Pembury Road, Tonbridge, Kent TN9 2JD.

Book 24. **A Guide to the Major Trusts.** Ed. Andrew Farrow and Luke Fitzherbert. 1993 edition. Directory of Social Change. £14.95. (Address above).

Book 25. **Government Grants: a guide for non-statutory organisations.** M.Jones. 1991. NCVO. £7.95. (Address above).

Book 26. **Grants from Europe: How to get money and influence policy.** Anne Davison and Bill Seary. Sixth Edition 1990. NCVO. £7.95. (Address above).

Other Information

The **Charities Aid Foundation** and "Accountancy" magazine jointly run the Charity Annual Report and Accounts Award. Prizes of up to £1000 can be won by the Charities producing clear, readable, annual reports, with well presented accounts. Charities Aid Foundation, 48 Pembury Road, Tonbridge, Kent TN9 2JD.

The **Charity Commission** provide advice and information to charities. Northern Office, Graeme House, Derby Square, Liverpool L2 7SB; or Central Register, St Alban's House, 57/60 Haymarket, London SW1Y 4QX.

Information on all aspects of volunteering can be obtained from the **Volunteer Centre UK**, 29 Lower King's Road, Berkhamsted, Herts, HP4 2AB.

The law affecting charities is different in Northern Ireland and Scotland. For more information contact:

- **Northern Ireland Council for Voluntary Action**, 127 Ormeau Road, Belfast, BT7 1SH.
- **Northern Ireland Charities Unit**, Department of Finance and Personnel, Room 255, Parliament Buildings, Stormont, Belfast BT4 3SW.
- **Scottish Council for Voluntary Organisations**, 19 Claremont Crescent, Edinburgh, EH7 4QD.

If you are a local organisation, you should first approach your nearest **Council for Voluntary Service or Rural Community Council** (in England), **County Voluntary Council** (in Wales) or **Council for Social Service** (in Scotland).

These organisations should be able to provide you with initial help and advice, and point you towards other sources of information.

COIF: the Charities Official Investment Fund and the Charities Deposit Fund are at St. Alphage House, 2, Fore Street, London EC2Y 5AQ.

Details of **CAFcash** and the **Charities Aid Foundation Covenant administration service** can be obtained from the Charities Aid Foundation (address above).

The **WM Company** can provide assessment of the performance of your organisation's investments. The WM Company, Lonsdale Chambers, 27 Chancery Lane, London, WC2A 1NF.

The **Institute of Charity Fundraising Managers** is promotes standards of practice among fundraisers. Write to ICFM, Market Towers, 1 Nine Elms Lane, Vauxhall, London SW8 5NQ.

ADDRESSES

Index

Aims	9	Priorities	14
Accounts		- setting	14
- annual	30	Promotion	25-26
- balance sheet	33	Record keeping	19-21
- examination of	34	Reporting	24-25
- income and expenditure	40-41	- requirements	18
- systems	32	Restricted income	39
Annual reports	24	Solvency	34
Assets	46-51	Tax effective giving	59
- cash	48	Values	7
- equipment	46	VAT	43
- investments	49	Volunteers, payments to	42
- property	47		
- stock	48		
Auditor	41		
Budgets	35-36		
Cash flow	38		
Deficit	34		
Evaluation	19-20		
- key features	22		
Financial terms	30-31		
Financial crisis	40		
Fundraising	52-59		
- committees	52		
- methods	54-55		
- plans and strategy	53		
Insurance	44		
Management information	23		
Management accounts	38-39		
Mission	9-10		
- statements	10		
Monitoring	19		
Need	6		
Objects	7-8		
- changing	8		
Objectives	9		
Outcomes	20		
Planning	12-13		
- types	12		
- day-to-day	15		
- strategic	12		
Policy	10		